Cooking Light

mix
& match
low-calorie
cookbook

ISBN-13: 978-0-8487-3408-4
ISBN-10: 0-8487-3408-4
Library of Congress Control Number: 2009941794
Printed in the United States of America
First Printing 2010

Be sure to check with your health-care provider before making any changes in your diet.

Oxmoor House
VP, Publishing Director: Jim Childs
Editorial Director: Susan Payne Dobbs
Brand Manager: Michelle Turner Aycock
Senior Editor: Heather Averett
Managing Editor: Laurie S. Herr

Cooking Light Mix & Match Low-Calorie Cookbook
Editor: Rachel Quinlivan, R.D.
Project Editor: Diane Rose
Director, Test Kitchens: Elizabeth Tyler Austin
Assistant Directors, Test Kitchens: Julie Christopher, Julie Gunter
Test Kitchens Professionals: Wendy Ball, Allison E. Cox, Victoria E. Cox, Alyson Moreland Haynes, Callie Nash, Kathleen Royal Phillips, Catherine Crowell Steele, Leah Van Deren
Photography Director: Jim Bathie
Senior Photo Stylist: Kay E. Clarke
Associate Photo Stylist: Katherine Eckert Coyne
Senior Production Manager: Greg A. Amason

Contributors
Designer and Compositor: Carol Damsky
Copy Editor: Dolores Hydock
Proofreader: Adrienne S. Davis
Indexer: Mary Ann Laurens
Interns: Sarah Bélanger, Christine T. Boatwright, Georgia Dodge, Caitlin Watzke

Cooking Light
Editor: Scott Mowbray
Creative Director: Carla Frank
Deputy Editor: Phillip Rhodes
Food Editor: Ann Taylor Pittman
Special Publications Editor: Mary Simpson Creel, M.S., R.D.
Nutrition Editor: Kathy Kitchens Downie, R.D.
Associate Food Editors: Timothy Q. Cebula, Julianna Grimes
Associate Editors: Cindy Hatcher, Brandy Rushing
Test Kitchen Director: Vanessa T. Pruett
Assistant Test Kitchen Director: Tiffany Vickers Davis
Chief Food Stylist: Charlotte Fekete
Senior Food Stylist: Kellie Gerber Kelley
Recipe Testers and Developers: Robin Bashinsky, Adam Hickman, Deb Wise
Art Director: Fernande Bondarenko
Junior Deputy Art Director: Alexander Spacher
Designer: Chase Turberville
Photo Director: Kristen Schaefer
Senior Photographer: Randy Mayor
Senior Photo Stylist: Cindy Barr
Photo Stylist: Leigh Ann Ross
Copy Chief: Maria Parker Hopkins
Assistant Copy Chief: Susan Roberts
Research Editor: Michelle Gibson Daniels
Editorial Production Director: Liz Rhoades
Production Editor: Hazel R. Eddins
Art/Production Assistant: Josh Rutledge
Administrative Coordinator: Carol D. Johnson
CookingLight.com Editor: Allison Long Lowery
CookingLight.com Nutrition Editor: Holley Johnson Grainger, M.S., R.D.
CookingLight.com Production Assistant: Mallory Daugherty

To order additional publications, call 1-800-765-6400 or 1-800-491-0551.

For more books to enrich your life, visit **oxmoorhouse.com**

To search, savor, and share thousands of recipes, visit **myrecipes.com**

Cover: Blueberry Pancakes (page 38); Grilled Turkey and Ham Sandwiches (page 140); Salmon with Maple-Lemon Glaze (page 164); Deep Dark Chocolate Biscotti (page 262); Lemonade Iced Tea Sorbet (page 294)

Back Cover (clockwise from top left): Morning Glory Muffins (page 34); Crisp and Spicy Snack Mix (page 254); Farfalle with Lamb Ragù, Ricotta, and Mint (page 194); Espresso Crinkles (page 272); BLT Bread Salad (page 96)

Cooking Light®

mix & match
low-calorie
cookbook

Oxmoor House®

contents

welcome

Maintaining a healthy weight (and losing weight, when needed) is part of a healthy lifestyle. And we know that it's the small choices you make on a daily basis that yield the biggest results over time—especially eating nutritious (and delicious) foods in the proper portions. But counting calories and writing down every bite you put in your mouth isn't ideal for the long term. *Cooking Light Mix & Match Low-Calorie Cookbook* was developed with that in mind.

The average woman needs about 1,500 calories a day to lose weight, and this book helps make it easier to meet that calorie goal each day. It's simple, really. This book is divided into four chapters: **Breakfast, Lunch, Dinner,** and **Snacks.** Each day, pick one recipe from the Breakfast chapter, one from Lunch, one from Dinner, and two from Snacks. No matter what the combination, the total will always equal 1,500 calories or less. And we haven't forgotten those of you with higher calorie needs—there's information throughout about how to healthfully add calories to your meals, too. Paired with tips on nutrition, exercise, and getting back on track when you've fallen off the healthy-eating wagon, the recipes in *Cooking Light Mix & Match Low-Calorie Cookbook* help you make living healthy essentially effortless.

The *Cooking Light* Editors

Cooking Light®
nutrition
made easy

Cooking Light
nutrition made easy

We know that when it comes to cooking and eating, it's the small choices that yield the biggest results over time. Therefore, we've included the following guidelines that sum up our thinking about nutrition and healthy cooking. They're healthy eating essentials that you'll find incorporated into the recipes throughout this book.

Cook More Often

Cooking at home means you are the nutritional gatekeeper of the kitchen; you control what your family eats. If you want to use less salt in a marinara to cut sodium; serve a dish incorporating more whole grains; or put a double layer of nutritious, leafy green spinach in your lasagna—that's your choice, and these recipes make it easy. You'll want to stock your pantry with healthy ingredients. You can easily pull a nutritious dinner together from well-stocked shelves and skip going to the grocery store or calling for pizza delivery.

Choose Healthy Fats

The old "less fat means a healthier diet" paradigm has been shifted by research suggesting that certain fats from vegetables, nuts, and fish actually promote good health. The fats you favor are just as important as how much you eat, so try to incorporate foods high in healthy fat—avocados, nuts, olives, vegetable oils, and canola-based mayonnaise—into your diet. Substitute plant-based fats for animal-based fats, when possible. For example, use canola oil in place of butter for sautéing vegetables. Choose fish loaded with omega-3 fatty acids, such as sardines, mackerel, sablefish, salmon, and rainbow trout a few times a week. Enjoy sensible portions of lean cuts of beef and pork as well as low-fat dairy to keep saturated fats in check. To avoid unhealthy trans fats, ignore the Nutrition Facts label and check the ingredient list: Partially hydrogenated oil of any kind means trans fats lurk within.

Select Carbs That Satisfy

Much confusion surrounds the topic of carbohydrates, thanks to fad diets that promote fat and protein over carbs. But like fats, it's the type of carbohydrates you choose that is the most important. All carbohydrates eventually turn to sugar in our bodies. These sugars give us the energy to perform tasks—from breathing to bicep curls. However, some carbohydrates convert to sugar more quickly than others. For this reason, nutrition recommendations for carbohydrates focus on complex carbohydrates, the more slowly digested kind found in whole grains, legumes, and vegetables (such as quinoa, kidney beans, and winter squash). They help you feel full and satisfied after a meal and keep your blood sugar levels more even, reducing the risk of developing type 2 diabetes.

Eat More Whole Foods

We don't yet know all the good things food processors are removing from what we eat. Although the list of nutrients on a nutrition label is short (fats, fiber, sugars, cholesterol, sodium, vitamins, etc.), the list of food components suspected of helping prevent disease is huge. Why is this important? Populations whose diets are based on whole foods tend to be less afflicted by diabetes, heart disease, and cancer. A diet rich in whole foods also tends to increase your consumption of fiber and complex carbohydrates and cuts your intake of simple sugars, refined carbs, and salt.

Save Room for Treats

Food is meant to be pleasurable, and part of the pleasure is treating yourself. Plus, a diet that doesn't include room for an occasional treat is not doable long term. Even the current version of the USDA Dietary Guidelines allows indulgences, providing a daily allotment that can be "spent" on treats—anything from a five-ounce glass of wine and a one-ounce square of chocolate to a scoop of ice cream or one of the two snacks we incorporate into our mix-and-match plan. If the rest of your diet includes smart options like fat-free milk and lean cuts of beef, plus plenty of produce and whole grains, you'll have room to enjoy these so-called "discretionary calories" as you wish.

Try Something New

Because life is short, the menu is long, and the odds favor the adventurous appetite: Variety ensures a nutrient-rich diet and, in our view, a much happier eater. By adventurous, we don't refer to the insect-munching stunt eaters of cable television but rather to expanding the types of foods you eat. It could be using bison instead of beef for your next burger or using Sriracha instead of traditional hot sauce or trying an unfamiliar dish at a local Indian restaurant. With the ever-expanding number of ethnic restaurants and grocery markets in the United States and the wide variety of ethnic cookbooks available, you're sure to find something new.

Eat Less Red and Processed Meat

Many processed meats contain nitrites, implicated in causing cancer. What's more, the compounds formed when meat, fish, or poultry are browned or charred have also been associated with disease. Large servings of red meat yield a diet high in saturated fat. And meat-centric eating pushes other healthy foods from the center of the plate to the side—or right off it. Eating less meat can be a challenge, though. Solutions include using meat for flavor rather than filler (a stir-fry of vegetables with thin slices of flank steak, for example); being creative with alternatives like tofu and beans (as creative as a home cook with a fussy family is allowed to be); and using small amounts of processed meats, such as prosciutto or bacon, as a flavoring or garnish.

Slash Sodium

For most people, the more sodium you consume, the higher your blood pressure will be. As blood pressure jumps, so does the risk of heart disease and stroke. The American Heart Association and the USDA Dietary Guidelines for Americans suggest limiting sodium to less than 2,300 milligrams a day (the amount in one teaspoon of salt) for healthy adults and 1,500 milligrams for those who are salt sensitive—typically individuals who have high blood pressure, are 40 years of age or older, or are African-American. Using these recipes helps keep sodium in check. Just watch the salt shaker.

Be Portion-Aware

The great secret of healthy eating is this: Once you know what constitutes the components of a good diet, you still need to be conscious of how much of those components to eat. Each of these recipes defines the serving size that keeps your calories under the daily limit. To further help you, use smaller plates, cups, and serving utensils—you'll dole out smaller portions. Use (or buy) a kitchen scale and measuring cups to portion food. With practice, you may be able to gauge a 4-ounce portion of beef or ½ cup of cooked vegetables by sight; until then, let the scale take the guesswork out of it. Purchase small containers of items like yogurt and 100 percent fruit juices. With packaged foods, be label-aware: One container, even a small one, doesn't necessarily mean one serving. Being deliberately and persistently aware of portion sizes is key until serving yourself proper portions becomes automatic. It's a necessary step toward healthier eating.

how to use
this book

Cooking Light Mix & Match Low-Calorie Cookbook is based on a **1,500**-calories-per-day diet—the amount the average woman needs to lose weight. The plan is simple: The book is divided into four recipe chapters, including **300**-calorie breakfasts, **400**-calorie lunches, **500**-calorie dinners, and **150**-calorie snacks. Simply choose one breakfast, one lunch, one dinner, and two snacks each day, and—no matter what the combination—the total will always be 1,500 calories or less.

Breakfast	300 calories
Lunch	400 calories
Dinner	500 calories
Snacks x 2	300 calories

=**1,500** calories

When needed, we've provided information about how to make these recipes a full meal. The calories for those suggestions have been added to the total calories found at the top of each page. For those who need extra calories (taller women, men, highly active individuals), we've provided information on every page about how to add additional calories to meet your needs in a healthful way—look for the text marked "a little more." For more information about your calorie needs, visit MyPyramid.gov.

We've also included "Back on Track" tips to help you refocus on your weight-loss and weight-maintenance goals and "Quick Fix" tips with information about ways to burn calories through exercise. All calorie estimates are based on a 150-pound person. If you weigh more, you'll burn more calories; if you weigh less, you'll burn fewer.

sample days

Carrot Cake Pancakes
244 calories

Cuban Sandwich
397 calories

Tilapia Tostadas with Roasted Corn Relish
470 calories

Spicy Black Bean Hummus with pita chips
148 calories

Vanilla Bean Shortbread
101 calories

1,360 calories

Scrambled Eggs with Morel and Tarragon Cream Sauce and salad
295 calories

BLT Bread Salad and fresh cantaloupe slices
362 calories

Cilantro-Lime Chicken with Avocado Salsa and saffron rice
485 calories

Crisp and Spicy Snack Mix
117 calories

Fudgy Mocha-Toffee Brownies
145 calories

1,404 calories

Oatmeal with Apples, Hazelnuts, and Flaxseed
258 calories

Butternut Squash Soup and salad
338 calories

Black Bean Burgers with Mango Salsa and veggie chips
470 calories

Mango Lassi
137 calories

Butterscotch Bars
148 calories

1,351 calories

breakfast

- Healthy Ideas to Start the Day
- Eating Out Tips
- Recipes

breakfast

The path to weight control and weight loss begins with a good breakfast, so start the day off with a healthy meal. Modern life is usually filled with deadlines and the hustle and bustle of daily activities, but good breakfast choices are not complicated or time-consuming. Indeed, morning offers the day's best opportunity to make whole grains, whole fruits, low-fat dairy, and other nutritious foods into a habit because breakfast tends to be a meal of habitual choices.

Why eat breakfast? People think they're cutting calories by skipping this morning meal, but consider a day without breakfast: By midmorning you have fasted for 12 hours or longer. This sets the stage for brain droop, maybe followed by some impulsive snacking. Lunch arrives and, over-hungry, you may eat too much, too fast. Or, if you have been "good," you may reach the dinner hour feeling you've earned a food "credit" after a stressful day—and then binge. And studies confirm that breakfast is essential when losing weight or maintaining weight loss. An impressive 78 percent of the 5,000 participants in the National Weight Control Registry (which tracks people's weight loss and maintenance success) report eating a regular breakfast—and they have lost an average of 66 pounds, maintaining that for more than five years.

Healthy Ideas to Start the Day

• **Make your own breakfast cereal** with rolled oats or kasha (buckwheat groats), dried fruits, and nuts. You'll gain all the nutrition benefits of a whole-grain, fruited cereal—free of crazy additives, sugary faux fruit bits, or refined grains.

• **Healthy savory leftovers can be a good option, too.** A piece of that veggie-rich pizza from the night before, or a slice of roast pork tenderloin tucked into 100 percent whole-grain bread, is a good savory option.

• **Sprinkle on nutrition with nutrient-rich wheat germ.** It's an old trick, but we love a little over yogurt or cold cereal or mix it into waffle and pancake batters.

• **Think outside the oat box.** Oats corner the market for hot, good-for-you cereals. But barley grits, rye flakes, or brown-rice cereals are interesting whole-grain updates on the old stand-by. Check health-food stores or supermarket cereal or baking aisles.

Eating Out Tips

Apply our healthy eating guidelines (starting on page 10) to the meals you eat outside of your house, too. For breakfast, watch out for added fats in the form of butter that are part of many drive-thru menus (choose an English muffin over a buttery biscuit), choose healthy condiments (peanut butter or jam is a better choice than gravy, butter, or syrups), and remember to always practice portion control. If drive-thru is the only option, here are some choices:

• *Egg McMuffin from McDonald's* = 300 calories
• *Perfect Oatmeal (140 calories) with brown sugar (50 calories) and either the dried fruit topping or the nut medley topping (both are 100 calories each) from Starbucks* = 290 calories
• *Au Bon Pain's Apple Cinnamon Oatmeal* = 280 calories

good choice:

1 whole-wheat English muffin + 1 tablespoon jam = 150 calories and 4 grams of filling fiber

not-so-good choice:

Glazed doughnut = 200 calories and less than 1 gram of fiber

Flaky Buttermilk Biscuits

These tender, old-fashioned biscuits are low in fat and flavored with buttermilk, butter, and a bit of honey.

9   ounces all-purpose flour (about 2 cups)
2½ teaspoons baking powder
½   teaspoon salt
5   tablespoons chilled butter, cut into small pieces
¾   cup fat-free buttermilk
3   tablespoons honey

1. Preheat oven to 400°.
2. Weigh or lightly spoon flour into dry measuring cups; level with a knife. Combine flour, baking powder, and salt in a large bowl; cut in butter with a pastry blender or 2 knives until mixture resembles coarse meal. Chill 10 minutes.
3. Combine buttermilk and honey, stirring with a whisk until well blended. Add buttermilk mixture to flour mixture; stir just until moist.
4. Turn dough out onto a lightly floured surface; knead lightly 4 times. Roll dough into a (½-inch-thick) 9 x 5–inch rectangle; dust top of dough with flour. Fold dough crosswise into thirds (as if folding a piece of paper to fit into an envelope). Re-roll dough into a (½-inch-thick) 9 x 5–inch rectangle; dust top of dough with flour. Fold dough crosswise into thirds; gently roll or pat to a ¾-inch thickness. Cut dough with a 1¾-inch biscuit cutter to form 14 dough rounds. Place dough rounds, 1 inch apart, on a baking sheet lined with parchment paper. Bake at 400° for 12 minutes or until golden. Remove from pan; cool 2 minutes on wire racks. Serve warm. **Yield:** 7 servings (serving size: 2 biscuits).

CALORIES 242; FAT 8.4g (sat 5.2g, mono 2.2g, poly 0.4g); PROTEIN 4.8g; CARB 36.8g; FIBER 1g; CHOL 22mg; IRON 1.8mg; SODIUM 396mg; CALC 126mg

Spiced Pumpkin Biscuits variation: Add 1¼ teaspoons pumpkin pie spice to flour mixture. Decrease buttermilk to ⅓ cup; add ¾ cup canned pumpkin to buttermilk mixture. Bake at 400° for 14 minutes. **Yield:** 7 servings (serving size: 2 biscuits).

CALORIES 244; FAT 8.6g (sat 5.2g, mono 2.2g, poly 0.4g); PROTEIN 4.6g; CARB 37.8g; FIBER 1.8g; CHOL 22mg; IRON 2.2mg; SODIUM 384mg; CALC 118mg

Parmesan-Pepper Biscuits variation: Add 1 teaspoon freshly ground black pepper to flour mixture. Decrease butter to ¼ cup. Add ½ cup (2 ounces) grated fresh Parmesan cheese to buttermilk mixture. Bake at 400° for 13 minutes. **Yield:** 7 servings (serving size: 2 biscuits).

CALORIES 262; FAT 9.4g (sat 5.8g, mono 1.8g, poly 0.4g); PROTEIN 8.4g; CARB 37g; FIBER 1g; CHOL 26mg; IRON 1.8mg; SODIUM 478mg; CALC 196mg

a little more...

Drizzle the biscuits with 1 tablespoon of honey for an additional 58 calories.

nutrition note

Biscuits

Biscuits are a great way to bring built-in portion control to the table. The ideal portion size for biscuits is about the size of a hockey puck (about 2 ounces), so place one serving on your plate, top with a bit of honey or jam (and a little butter if you like), and don't go back for seconds.

Sweet Potato Biscuits

Cutting in the butter makes for flaky, delicate biscuits. Be sure to stop cutting in the butter while there are still pebble-sized pieces. If you work it longer, the biscuits will be tough.

9 ounces all-purpose flour (about 2 cups)
1 tablespoon sugar
2 teaspoons baking powder
½ teaspoon salt
5 tablespoons chilled unsalted butter, cut into small pieces
1 cup pureed cooked sweet potatoes, cooled
⅓ cup fat-free milk
Cooking spray

1. Preheat oven to 400°.
2. Weigh or lightly spoon flour into dry measuring cups; level with a knife. Combine flour, sugar, baking powder, and salt in a bowl. Cut in butter with a pastry blender or 2 knives until mixture resembles coarse meal. Combine sweet potato and milk in a small bowl; add potato mixture to flour mixture, stirring just until moist.
3. Turn dough out onto a lightly floured surface, and knead lightly 5 times. Roll dough to a ¾-inch thickness; cut with a 2-inch biscuit cutter into 10 biscuits. Place biscuits on a baking sheet coated with cooking spray. Gather remaining dough. Roll to a ¾-inch thickness. Cut with a 2-inch biscuit cutter into 6 biscuits. Place biscuits on prepared baking sheet. Discard any remaining scraps.
4. Bake at 400° for 15 minutes or until lightly browned. Remove from pan; cool 5 minutes on wire racks. Serve warm or at room temperature. **Yield:** 8 servings (serving size: 2 biscuits).

CALORIES 248; FAT 7.4g (sat 4.6g, mono 1.8g, poly 0.4g); PROTEIN 4.6g; CARB 40.2g; FIBER 2.6g; CHOL 20mg; IRON 2mg; SODIUM 346mg; CALC 94mg

a little more...

Serve the biscuits with 2 teaspoons of Maple Butter for an additional 64 calories per serving.

Maple Butter

Serve this butter chilled, or let it stand at room temperature about 20 minutes to soften. It's also great with corn bread, pancakes, or waffles.

6 tablespoons butter, softened
3 tablespoons maple syrup
⅛ teaspoon salt

1. Combine all ingredients in a small bowl; beat with a mixer at medium speed 1 minute or until smooth. Cover and chill until ready to serve. **Yield:** 24 servings (serving size: 1 teaspoon).

CALORIES 32; FAT 2.8g (sat 1.8g, mono 0.7g, poly 0.1g); PROTEIN 0g; CARB 1.7g; FIBER 0g; CHOL 8mg; IRON 0mg; SODIUM 33mg; CALC 3mg

nutrition note

Sweet Potatoes

Sweet potatoes are loaded with beta-carotene, a compound that gives them their intense orange color and also acts as an antioxidant. They're also a good source of fiber; potassium; and vitamins A, C, and E.

Banana Bran Scones

Banana brings a light, fruity sweetness to these spiced scones. You can prepare them for brunch or to have on hand as an evening snack with hot chocolate. Serve with 1 cup of fresh blackberries (62 calories) to complete your breakfast.

230 calories

4.5   ounces all-purpose flour
      (about 1 cup)
½   cup oat bran
2   tablespoons chilled butter, cut into
    small pieces
1   teaspoon baking powder
¼   teaspoon baking soda
¼   teaspoon salt
¼   teaspoon ground cinnamon
¾   cup ripe mashed banana (about 2)
1   tablespoon light brown sugar
¼   cup nonfat buttermilk
1½   teaspoons nonfat buttermilk
1½   teaspoons granulated sugar

1. Preheat oven to 400°.
2. Weigh or lightly spoon flour into a dry measuring cup; level with a knife. Combine flour and next 6 ingredients in a food processor; pulse until mixture resembles coarse meal.
3. Combine banana and brown sugar in a medium bowl; let stand 5 minutes.

Add flour mixture and ¼ cup buttermilk alternately to banana mixture, stirring just until moist.
4. Turn dough out onto a lightly floured surface; knead lightly 1½ minutes with floured hands. Pat dough into a 6-inch circle on a baking sheet lined with parchment paper. Cut dough into 6 wedges, cutting into, but not through, dough. Brush 1½ teaspoons buttermilk over surface of dough; sprinkle with granulated sugar. Bake at 400° for 12 minutes or until lightly browned. Remove from pan; cool on wire racks. **Yield:** 6 servings (serving size: 1 scone).

CALORIES 168; FAT 4.7g (sat 2.5g, mono 1.2g, poly 0.5g); PROTEIN 4.3g; CARB 30.9g; FIBER 2.5g; CHOL 11mg; IRON 1.6mg; SODIUM 272mg; CALC 72mg

a little more...

Top your scone with 2 teaspoons of butter (67 calories) or your favorite flavor of jam (50 calories).

nutrition note

Oat Bran

There are three main parts of grains: the bran, germ, and endosperm. Oat bran is the outer husk of the oat grain and is designed to protect the grain and provide nutrition until it can sprout. It contains the bulk of the dietary fiber of the grain plus minerals. When added to baked goods, it adds a distinct grainy texture and rich, nutty flavor. You can also add it to cereals for a hefty boost of fiber.

Blueberry-Pecan Scones

Make these scones a day or two ahead, and store in an airtight container. Resist the temptation to knead the dough; doing so would break apart the tender blueberries. Leftover scones are nice with tea later in the day.

½ cup 2% reduced-fat milk
¼ cup sugar
2 teaspoons grated lemon rind
1 teaspoon vanilla extract
1 large egg
9 ounces all-purpose flour (about 2 cups)
1 tablespoon baking powder
½ teaspoon salt
3 tablespoons chilled butter, cut into small pieces
1 cup fresh or frozen blueberries
¼ cup finely chopped pecans, toasted
Cooking spray
1 large egg white, lightly beaten
2 tablespoons sugar

1. Preheat oven to 375°.
2. Combine first 5 ingredients in a medium bowl, stirring with a whisk. Weigh or lightly spoon flour into dry measuring cups; level with a knife. Combine flour, baking powder, and salt in a large bowl, stirring with a whisk. Cut in butter with a pastry blender or 2 knives until mixture resembles coarse meal. Gently fold in blueberries and pecans. Add milk mixture, stirring just until moist (dough will be sticky).
3. Turn dough out onto a floured surface; pat dough into an 8-inch circle. Cut dough into 10 wedges, and place the dough wedges on a baking sheet coated with cooking spray. Brush egg white over dough wedges; sprinkle evenly with 2 tablespoons sugar. Bake scones at 375° for 18 minutes or until golden. Serve warm. **Yield:** 10 servings (serving size: 1 scone).

CALORIES 196; FAT 6.6g (sat 2.2g, mono 2.9g, poly 1g); PROTEIN 4.4g; CARB 30.2g; FIBER 1.4g; CHOL 31mg; IRON 1.5mg; SODIUM 308mg; CALC 107mg

a little more...

If you'd like larger portions, cut the scones into 8 wedges before baking. You'll get a heftier wedge weighing in at 245 calories per scone.

nutrition note

Blueberries

Blueberries are packed with antioxidants that offer a variety of health benefits. They're also an excellent source of vitamin C and a good source of fiber.

Whole-Wheat, Oatmeal, and Raisin Muffins

204 calories

Adding boiling water to the batter and allowing it to sit for 15 minutes before baking allows the hearty oats, wheat germ, and bran to soak up the liquid for a more tender muffin.

4.75 ounces whole-wheat flour (about 1 cup)
¼ cup granulated sugar
¼ cup packed brown sugar
2 tablespoons untoasted wheat germ
2 tablespoons wheat bran
1½ teaspoons baking soda
1 teaspoon ground cinnamon
½ teaspoon salt
1½ cups quick-cooking oats
⅓ cup chopped pitted dates
⅓ cup raisins
⅓ cup dried cranberries
1 cup low-fat buttermilk
¼ cup canola oil
1 teaspoon vanilla extract
1 large egg, lightly beaten
½ cup boiling water
Cooking spray

1. Weigh or lightly spoon flour into a dry measuring cup; level with a knife. Combine flour and next 7 ingredients in a large bowl, stirring with a whisk. Stir in oats and next 3 ingredients. Make a well in center of mixture. Combine buttermilk and next 3 ingredients; add to flour mixture, stirring just until moist. Stir in ½ cup boiling water. Let batter stand 15 minutes.

2. Preheat oven to 375°.

3. Spoon batter into 12 muffin cups coated with cooking spray. Bake at 375° for 20 minutes or until muffins spring back when touched lightly in center. Remove muffins from pans immediately; place on a wire rack. **Yield:** 12 servings (serving size: 1 muffin).

CALORIES 204; FAT 6.4g (sat 0.8g, mono 3.2g, poly 1.8g); PROTEIN 4.6g; CARB 34.7g; FIBER 3.4g; CHOL 19mg; IRON 1.4mg; SODIUM 288mg; CALC 43mg

a little more...

Pair one of these muffins with a 1-cup glass of orange juice for an additional 110 calories.

nutrition note

Healthy Fillings

With four whole grains—whole-wheat flour, wheat germ, wheat bran, and oats—and three dried fruits, these muffins are a great way to get a variety of antioxidants and fiber.

Orange-Cranberry Wheat Germ Muffins

197 calories

These muffins are at their best warm, so reheat briefly if you make them ahead.

6.75   **ounces all-purpose flour (about 1½ cups)**
- ½   **cup raw wheat germ**
- ½   **cup sweetened dried cranberries**
- 1   **teaspoon baking powder**
- ½   **teaspoon baking soda**
- ½   **teaspoon ground cinnamon**
- ¼   **teaspoon salt**
- ⅛   **teaspoon ground nutmeg**
- ¾   **cup packed brown sugar**
- ¼   **cup canola oil**
- 1   **teaspoon grated orange rind**
- ½   **cup fresh orange juice**
- 2   **large eggs**
    Cooking spray
- 1   **tablespoon turbinado sugar**

1. Preheat oven to 375°.
2. Weigh or lightly spoon flour into dry measuring cups; level with a knife. Combine flour and next 7 ingredients in a large bowl; stir with a whisk. Make a well in center of mixture.
3. Combine brown sugar, oil, rind, juice, and eggs; stir with a whisk. Add egg mixture to flour mixture; stir just until combined. Spoon batter into 12 muffin cups coated with cooking spray. Sprinkle with turbinado sugar. Bake at 375° for 17 minutes or until muffins spring back when touched lightly in center. **Yield:** 12 servings (serving size: 1 muffin).

CALORIES 197; FAT 5.8g (sat 0.6g, mono 3.1g, poly 1.6g); PROTEIN 3.4g; CARB 33.8g; FIBER 1.2g; CHOL 35mg; IRON 1.7mg; SODIUM 149mg; CALC 54mg

a little more...

Split a muffin in two and spread 1 tablespoon of peanut butter between the two for an additional 90 calories.

nutrition note

Wheat Germ

Wheat germ, which is made from the wheat kernel, is an excellent source of vitamin E, is high in protein, and contains 23 nutrients—more nutrients per ounce than any other vegetable or grain, including more potassium and iron than any other food source.

Morning Glory Muffins

256 calories

Substitute apricots or raisins for chopped pitted dates in this recipe if you like. The dried fruits, nuts, oatmeal, wheat bran, and whole-wheat flour contribute plenty of fiber to each morning glory muffin. Complete your breakfast with cantaloupe wedges—a serving of 3 wedges contains 70 calories.

Cooking spray
4.75 ounces whole-wheat flour (about 1 cup)
2.25 ounces all-purpose flour (about ½ cup)
1 cup regular oats
¾ cup packed brown sugar
1 tablespoon wheat bran
2 teaspoons baking soda
¼ teaspoon salt
1 cup plain fat-free yogurt
1 cup mashed ripe banana (about 2)
1 large egg
1 cup chopped pitted dates
¾ cup chopped walnuts
½ cup chopped dried pineapple
3 tablespoons ground flaxseed (about 2 tablespoons whole)

1. Preheat oven to 350°.
2. Place 18 paper muffin cup liners in muffin cups; coat liners with cooking spray.

3. Weigh or lightly spoon flours into dry measuring cups; level with a knife. Combine flours and next 5 ingredients in a large bowl; stir with a whisk. Make a well in center of mixture.
4. Combine yogurt, banana, and egg; add to flour mixture, stirring just until moist. Fold in dates, walnuts, and pineapple. Spoon batter into prepared muffin cups. Sprinkle evenly with flaxseed.
5. Bake at 350° for 20 minutes or until muffins spring back when touched lightly in center. Remove muffins from pans immediately; cool on a wire rack. **Yield:** 18 servings (serving size: 1 muffin).

CALORIES 186; FAT 4.4g (sat 0.5g, mono 0.7g, poly 2.8g); PROTEIN 4.2g; CARB 35.2g; FIBER 3.4g; CHOL 12mg; IRON 1.2mg; SODIUM 190mg; CALC 42mg

a little more...

Add a 6-ounce carton of fat-free yogurt for an additional 100 calories.

quick fix

Ride Your Bike

During a leisurely (less than 10 miles per hour) 30-minute bike ride, you can burn about 140 calories. Amp up the intensity to more than 10 miles per hour, and you can double the amount of calories you burn.

Bacon-Cheddar Corn Muffins

Use extrasharp cheese for the most intense flavor. These muffins are great for breakfast or with soup. Split the muffins in two and toast for tasty leftovers.

284 calories

Cooking spray
- 6.75 ounces all-purpose flour (about 1½ cups)
- ½ cup yellow cornmeal
- 1 teaspoon baking powder
- 1 teaspoon baking soda
- 1 teaspoon sugar
- ½ teaspoon salt
- 1 cup fat-free milk
- 2 tablespoons lemon juice
- 2 tablespoons butter, melted
- 1 large egg
- ½ cup (2 ounces) shredded extrasharp cheddar cheese
- 4 center-cut bacon slices, cooked and crumbled

1. Preheat oven to 400°.
2. Place 12 paper muffin cup liners in muffin cups. Coat liners with cooking spray; set aside.
3. Weigh or lightly spoon flour into dry measuring cups; level with a knife. Combine flour and next 5 ingredients in a large bowl; make a well in center of mixture.
4. Combine milk and juice in a medium bowl; let stand 2 minutes (milk will curdle). Add butter and egg; stir well to combine. Add to flour mixture, stirring just until moist. Stir in cheese and bacon. Spoon batter evenly into prepared muffin cups. Bake at 400° for 17 minutes or until muffins spring back when touched lightly in center. Remove muffins from pans immediately; place on a wire rack. **Yield:** 6 servings (serving size: 2 muffins).

CALORIES 284; FAT 9.6g (sat 5.2g, mono 3g, poly 0.6g); PROTEIN 10.4g; CARB 38.2g; FIBER 1.2g; CHOL 60mg; IRON 2.2mg; SODIUM 684mg; CALC 176mg

a little more...

Add a cup of cubed honeydew for an additional 60 calories.

nutrition note

Center-Cut Bacon

This type of bacon has the same satisfying flavor, but because it's cut closer to the bone, it contains about 20 percent less saturated fat than regular bacon. A serving of two slices is modest in calories (40 calories) and saturated fat (1 gram), plus the sodium is reasonable (173 milligrams).

Blueberry Pancakes

Since these pancakes reheat well in the toaster oven, you can make a big batch and enjoy them all week.

272 calories

- **2.25 ounces all-purpose flour (about ½ cup)**
- **2.4 ounces whole-wheat flour (about ½ cup)**
- **1 tablespoon sugar**
- **1 teaspoon baking powder**
- **½ teaspoon baking soda**
- **⅛ teaspoon salt**
- **⅛ teaspoon ground nutmeg**
- **¾ cup vanilla fat-free yogurt**
- **2 tablespoons butter, melted**
- **2 teaspoons fresh lemon juice**
- **½ teaspoon vanilla extract**
- **2 large eggs, lightly beaten**
- **Cooking spray**
- **1 cup fresh blueberries**

1. Weigh or lightly spoon flours into dry measuring cups; level with a knife. Combine flours and next 5 ingredients in a large bowl, stirring well with a whisk. Combine yogurt and next 4 ingredients in a small bowl; add to flour mixture, stirring until smooth.

2. Heat a large nonstick skillet over medium heat. Coat pan with cooking spray. Pour about ¼ cup batter per pancake onto a hot nonstick griddle or nonstick skillet. Top each pancake with 2 tablespoons blueberries. Cook 2 minutes or until tops are covered with bubbles and edges look cooked. Carefully turn pancakes over; cook 2 minutes or until bottoms are lightly browned. **Yield:** 4 servings (serving size: 2 pancakes).

CALORIES 272; FAT 8.8g (sat 4.5g, mono 2.5g, poly 0.8g); PROTEIN 9.5g; CARB 40.1g; FIBER 3.2g; CHOL 122mg; IRON 2mg; SODIUM 403mg; CALC 192mg

a little more...

Add a cup of fresh strawberries for an additional 50 calories. For a special treat, you can substitute ½ cup of chocolate chips for the fresh blueberries. The calories per serving will increase to 411 calories.

quick fix

Running

Lace up your sneakers for a run (at a pace of 10 minutes per mile) and you'll burn about 350 calories in 30 minutes.

Carrot Cake Pancakes

These cakey flapjacks feature warm spices and bright carrot flavor. Our lightened version uses low-fat buttermilk in the pancakes.

5.6	ounces all-purpose flour (about 1¼ cups)
¼	cup chopped walnuts, toasted
2	teaspoons baking powder
1	teaspoon ground cinnamon
¼	teaspoon salt
⅛	teaspoon freshly ground nutmeg
	Dash of ground cloves
	Dash of ground ginger
¼	cup packed brown sugar
¾	cup low-fat buttermilk
1	tablespoon canola oil
1½	teaspoons vanilla extract
2	large eggs, lightly beaten
2	cups finely grated carrot (about 1 pound)
	Cooking spray

1. Weigh or lightly spoon flour into dry measuring cups; level with a knife. Combine flour and next 7 ingredients in a large bowl, stirring with a whisk. Combine ¼ cup brown sugar and next 4 ingredients; add sugar mixture to flour mixture, stirring just until moist. Fold in 2 cups carrot.

2. Heat a large nonstick skillet over medium heat. Coat pan with cooking spray. Pour about ¼ cup batter per pancake onto a hot nonstick griddle or nonstick skillet; spread gently with a spatula. Cook 2 minutes or until tops are covered with bubbles and edges look cooked. Carefully turn pancakes over; cook 1 minute or until bottoms are lightly browned. Repeat procedure twice with remaining batter. **Yield:** 6 servings (serving size: 2 pancakes).

CALORIES 244; FAT 7.6g (sat 1.2g, mono 2.9g, poly 3.1g); PROTEIN 7.7g; CARB 35.8g; FIBER 2.2g; CHOL 63mg; IRON 2.3mg; SODIUM 340mg; CALC 175mg

a little more...

Combine 3 tablespoons softened butter and 2 tablespoons honey in a small bowl to create a tasty honey butter to serve with your pancakes. A 2-teaspoon serving will add 71 calories to your meal.

nutrition note

Carrots

With their crunchy texture and sweet flavor, carrots can be a welcome addition to quick breads. Nutritionally, they offer a host of benefits. They're an excellent source of a variety of antioxidants, and the richest vegetable source of carotenes. These compounds help protect against heart disease and cancer and also promote good vision, particularly night vision.

Coconut Pancakes

3.33   ounces all-purpose flour (about ¾ cup)
1   ounce coconut flour or all-purpose flour (about ⅓ cup)
1½   teaspoons baking powder
1½   teaspoons granulated sugar
¼   teaspoon salt
1   cup light coconut milk
¼   cup fat-free milk
1   tablespoon canola oil
1   large egg
Cooking spray

1. Weigh or lightly spoon flours into dry measuring cups; level with a knife. Combine flours, baking powder, granulated sugar, and salt in a large bowl. Combine coconut milk and next 3 ingredients in a small bowl, stirring with a whisk. Add milk mixture to flour mixture, stirring with a whisk (batter will be thick).

2. Heat a large nonstick skillet over medium heat. Coat pan with cooking spray. Pour about ¼ cup batter per pancake onto a hot nonstick griddle or nonstick skillet; spread gently with a spatula. Cook 2 minutes or until tops are covered with bubbles and edges look cooked. Carefully turn pancakes over; cook 2 minutes or until bottoms are lightly browned. **Yield:** 4 servings (serving size: 2 pancakes).

CALORIES 241; FAT 9.1g (sat 4.3g, mono 2.5g, poly 1.3g); PROTEIN 7g; CARB 34.6g; FIBER 6.6g; CHOL 53mg; IRON 2.1mg; SODIUM 373mg; CALC 142mg

a little more...

Serve the pancakes with about ½ cup of Orange-Mango Compote for an additional 89 calories per serving.

Orange-Mango Compote

The compote is a delicious topping for pancakes, French toast, or oatmeal. It keeps well in the fridge for several days.

1½   cups chopped cored peeled red apple (about 1 medium)
1   cup chopped peeled mango (about 1 medium)
1   cup water
1   teaspoon grated orange rind
⅓   cup chopped orange sections
2   tablespoons light brown sugar
¼   teaspoon ground cinnamon
1   tablespoon cornstarch
1   tablespoon water
1½   teaspoons fresh lime juice

1. Combine first 7 ingredients in a large saucepan; bring to a boil. Cover, reduce heat, and cook 8 minutes or until fruit is tender. Combine cornstarch, 1 tablespoon water, and lime juice in a small bowl, stirring with a whisk; stir into fruit mixture, and bring to a boil. Cook 1 minute or until slightly thickened, stirring constantly. Remove from heat. **Yield:** 4 servings (serving size: about ½ cup).

CALORIES 89; FAT 0.2g (sat 0g, mono 0.1g, poly 0g); PROTEIN 0.5g; CARB 23g; FIBER 1.8g; CHOL 0mg; IRON 0.3mg; SODIUM 4mg; CALC 21mg

back on track

Sign Up for a Race

To get back on track, sign up for a race with a friend and train together. It's hard to skip exercise when a friend is counting on you to be there too. Plus, once you've paid the registration fee for the race, you're less likely to let that money go to waste.

Banana-Cinnamon Waffles

These lightly spiced waffles are topped with sliced bananas and maple syrup, but if you'd prefer them without these additions, a plain serving contains 215 calories.

4.5 ounces all-purpose flour (about 1 cup)
2.4 ounces whole-wheat flour (about ½ cup)
1 ounce buckwheat flour (about ¼ cup)
¼ cup ground flaxseed
2 tablespoons sugar
1½ teaspoons baking powder
½ teaspoon ground cinnamon
¼ teaspoon salt
1½ cups fat-free milk
3 tablespoons butter, melted
2 large eggs, lightly beaten
1 large ripe banana, mashed
Cooking spray
½ cup maple syrup
2 large bananas, cut into slices

1. Weigh or lightly spoon flours into dry measuring cups; level with a knife. Combine flours, flaxseed, and next 4 ingredients in a medium bowl, stirring with a whisk.

2. Combine milk, butter, and eggs, stirring with a whisk; add milk mixture to flour mixture, stirring until blended. Fold in mashed banana.

3. Preheat a waffle iron. Coat iron with cooking spray. Spoon about ¼ cup batter per 4-inch waffle onto hot waffle iron, spreading batter to edges. Cook 3 to 4 minutes or until steaming stops; repeat procedure with remaining batter. Drizzle each serving with maple syrup and top with banana slices. **Yield:** 8 servings (serving size: 2 waffles, 1 tablespoon syrup, and about ¼ cup banana slices).

CALORIES 297; FAT 7.6g (sat 3.4g, mono 1.9g, poly 1.4g); PROTEIN 7.7g; CARB 52.3g; FIBER 4.3g; CHOL 65mg; IRON 2.2mg; SODIUM 207mg; CALC 148mg

a little more...

Top these waffles with an extra ¼ cup of banana slices for an extra 30 calories and an additional gram of fiber.

nutrition note

Buckwheat Flour

Buckwheat flour provides protein and fiber. It has an assertive flavor adding a somewhat tangy, robust nuttiness to both quick and yeast breads.

Gingerbread Waffles

293 calories

Top these fluffy waffles with 1 teaspoon of butter (33 calories) and 1 tablespoon of maple syrup (52 calories).

- **9 ounces all-purpose flour (about 2 cups)**
- **1½ teaspoons baking powder**
- **½ teaspoon baking soda**
- **¼ teaspoon salt**
- **¼ teaspoon ground cinnamon**
- **1½ cups fat-free buttermilk**
- **3 tablespoons canola oil**
- **3 tablespoons molasses**
- **2 teaspoons finely grated peeled fresh ginger**
- **2 large egg yolks**
- **1 (4-ounce) container applesauce**
- **3 tablespoons minced crystallized ginger**
- **2 large egg whites**
- **Cooking spray**

1. Weigh or lightly spoon flour into dry measuring cups; level with a knife. Combine flour, baking powder, and next 3 ingredients in a medium bowl; stir with a whisk. Combine buttermilk and next 5 ingredients in a small bowl. Add milk mixture to flour mixture, stirring just until combined. Stir in crystallized ginger.

2. Beat egg whites with a mixer at high speed until soft peaks form. Gently fold egg whites into batter.

3. Preheat a Belgian waffle iron. Coat iron with cooking spray. Spoon about ⅔ cup batter per 4-inch waffle onto hot Belgian waffle iron, spreading batter to edges. Cook 5 minutes or until steaming stops; repeat procedure with remaining batter.

Yield: 9 servings (serving size: 1 waffle).

Note: You can use a regular waffle iron if you like. Simply spoon ⅓ cup batter per 4-inch waffle onto a hot waffle iron. A serving will be 2 waffles. The nutrition information per serving is the same.

CALORIES 208; FAT 6.1g (sat 0.7g, mono 3.2g, poly 1.7g); PROTEIN 5.8g; CARB 32.5g; FIBER 1g; CHOL 47mg; IRON 2mg; SODIUM 277mg; CALC 124mg

a little more...

Add ¾ cup of grapes for an additional 90 calories. For something special, substitute 2 tablespoons of lemon curd in place of the syrup and butter. It'll provide a sweet punch of flavor to each waffle and add 130 calories to your meal, bringing a serving to 338 calories.

nutrition note

Canola Oil

An ideal all-purpose oil is low in saturated fats and high in mono- and poly-unsaturated fats. One of our favorites that meets this criteria is canola oil. It has the least amount of saturated fat of any cooking oil (only 7 percent), and its mild flavor makes it ideal for a wide range of uses.

Marmalade French Toast Casserole

Grapefruit or mixed fruit marmalade will work just as well as the orange marmalade called for in the recipe. Serve the casserole with honey or pancake syrup warmed with orange rind and a splash of orange juice (add 1 teaspoon rind and 2 tablespoons juice per ½ cup syrup). This easy casserole can be assembled in less than 15 minutes before being stored in the refrigerator overnight.

   3   **tablespoons butter, softened**
   1   **(16-ounce) sourdough French bread loaf, cut into 24 (½-inch) slices**
       Cooking spray
   1   **(12-ounce) jar orange marmalade**
  2¾   **cups 1% low-fat milk**
   ⅓   **cup sugar**
   1   **teaspoon vanilla extract**
   ¼   **teaspoon ground nutmeg**
   6   **large eggs**
   ⅓   **cup finely chopped walnuts**

1. Spread softened butter on 1 side of each bread slice. Arrange 12 bread slices, buttered sides down, slightly overlapping in a single layer in a 13 x 9–inch baking dish coated with cooking spray. Spread marmalade evenly over bread; top with remaining 12 bread slices, buttered sides up.

2. Combine milk and next 4 ingredients, stirring with a whisk. Pour egg mixture over bread. Cover and refrigerate 8 hours or overnight.

3. Preheat oven to 350°.

4. Sprinkle casserole with walnuts. Bake at 350° for 45 minutes or until golden. Let stand 5 minutes before serving. Cut into 12 pieces. **Yield:** 12 servings (serving size: 1 piece).

CALORIES 293; FAT 9g (sat 3.2g, mono 2.2g, poly 2.3g); PROTEIN 9.1g; CARB 46.4g; FIBER 1.6g; CHOL 116mg; IRON 2.2mg; SODIUM 315mg; CALC 132mg

a little more...

If you'd like a more ample portion, cut this casserole into 9 pieces—each serving will contain 389 calories. Or, serve with orange sections. A medium orange contains about 60 calories.

nutrition note

Marmalade

Marmalade is a fruit preserve that includes pieces of the rind in the jelly base. It's primarily made from citrus fruits, particularly oranges, and because it contains both the rind and the flesh, it has a sour, bitter flavor unlike other jams and jellies.

Whole-Wheat Cinnamon Rolls

Pair these sweet rolls with 2 pieces of center-cut bacon (40 calories) to round out this weekend-worthy meal.

249 calories

1½ packages dry yeast (about 3¼ teaspoons)
¾ cup warm fat-free milk (100° to 110°)
¼ cup warm water (100° to 110°)
¼ cup butter, softened
¼ cup honey
½ teaspoon salt
1½ teaspoons fresh lemon juice
1 large egg
1 large egg white
11.25 ounces all-purpose flour (about 2½ cups), divided
7 ounces whole-wheat flour (about 1½ cups)
Cooking spray
¼ cup packed brown sugar
1½ tablespoons ground cinnamon
⅛ teaspoon ground nutmeg
⅓ cup raisins
¾ cup powdered sugar, sifted
¾ teaspoon vanilla extract
5 teaspoons fat-free milk

1. Dissolve yeast in warm milk and ¼ cup warm water in a large bowl; let stand 5 minutes or until foamy. Add butter and next 5 ingredients; stir well. Weigh or lightly spoon flours into dry measuring cups; level with a knife. Add 9 ounces all-purpose flour (about 2 cups) and whole-wheat flour to yeast mixture, stirring until a soft dough forms. Turn dough out onto a floured surface. Knead until smooth and elastic (about 8 minutes); add enough of remaining 2.25 ounces all-purpose flour (about ½ cup), 1 tablespoon at a time, to prevent dough from sticking to hands (dough will feel sticky). Place dough in a large bowl coated with cooking spray, turning to coat top. Cover and let rise in a warm place (85°), free from drafts, 1 hour or until doubled in size. (Gently press two fingers into dough. If indentation remains, dough has risen enough.) Punch dough down; roll into a 16 x 12–inch rectangle on a floured surface. Coat surface of dough with cooking spray.

2. Combine brown sugar, cinnamon, and nutmeg; sprinkle over dough, leaving a ½-inch border. Sprinkle raisins over dough, pressing gently into dough. Roll up rectangle tightly, starting with a long edge, pressing firmly to eliminate air pockets; pinch seam to seal. Cut dough into 16 rolls. Place rolls, cut sides up, in a 13 x 9–inch baking pan coated with cooking spray. Cover and let rise 45 minutes or until doubled in size.

3. Preheat oven to 375°.

4. Uncover rolls. Bake at 375° for 22 minutes or until lightly browned. Cool in pan on a wire rack.

5. Place powdered sugar and vanilla in a small bowl. Add 5 teaspoons milk, 1 teaspoon at a time, stirring to form a thick glaze. Drizzle glaze evenly over rolls. **Yield:** 16 servings (serving size: 1 roll).

CALORIES 209; FAT 3.7g (sat 2g, mono 0.9g, poly 0.3g); PROTEIN 5.1g; CARB 40.4g; FIBER 2.6g; CHOL 21mg; IRON 2mg; SODIUM 111mg; CALC 39mg

a little more…

Double up on these sweet rolls for a more substantial breakfast.

nutrition note

Weighing Flour

Measuring flour is the most important part of successful light baking—too much flour will yield a dry product. Because of this, we list the flour amounts in our ingredient lists by weight and approximate cup measure for those who don't have a kitchen scale. It's preferable to measure by weight because it's more accurate and ensures you'll get the same delicious results we achieve in our Test Kitchens. If you use measuring cups be sure to stir the flour in the canister before spooning it out, lightly spoon the flour into the measuring cup (do not pack it in), and then level off the excess with a knife.

Pecan Sticky Rolls

- ¾ cup warm fat-free milk (100° to 110°)
- ¼ cup granulated sugar
- ½ teaspoon salt
- 1 package dry yeast (about 2¼ teaspoons)
- ¼ cup warm water (100° to 110°)
- ½ cup egg substitute
- 3 tablespoons butter, melted and cooled
- 18 ounces all-purpose flour (about 4 cups), divided
- Cooking spray
- ¾ cup packed dark brown sugar
- 3 tablespoons butter, melted
- 2 tablespoons hot water
- ⅓ cup finely chopped pecans, toasted
- ⅔ cup granulated sugar
- 1 tablespoon ground cinnamon
- 1½ tablespoons butter, melted

1. Combine first 3 ingredients in a bowl.
2. Dissolve yeast in ¼ cup warm water in a small bowl; let stand 5 minutes. Stir yeast mixture into milk mixture. Add egg substitute and 3 tablespoons melted butter; stir until well combined.
3. Weigh or lightly spoon flour into dry measuring cups; level with a knife. Add 16.8 ounces (about 3¾ cups) flour to yeast mixture; stir until smooth. Turn dough out onto a lightly floured surface. Knead until smooth and elastic (about 8 minutes); add enough of remaining flour, 1 tablespoon at a time, to prevent dough from sticking to hands (dough will feel slightly soft and tacky).
4. Place dough in a large bowl coated with cooking spray; turn to coat top. Cover and let rise in a warm place (85°), free from drafts, 45 minutes. Punch dough down and turn over in bowl; lightly coat with cooking spray. Cover and let rise 45 minutes. Punch dough down; cover and let rest 5 minutes.
5. Combine brown sugar, 3 tablespoons butter, and 2 tablespoons hot water in a small bowl; stir with a whisk until smooth. Scrape sugar mixture into a 13 x 9–inch baking pan coated with cooking spray, spreading evenly over bottom of pan with a spatula. Sprinkle sugar mixture evenly with pecans, and set aside.
6. Combine ⅔ cup granulated sugar and cinnamon in a small bowl. Turn dough out onto a lightly floured surface; pat dough into a 16 x 12–inch rectangle. Brush surface of dough with 1½ tablespoons melted butter. Sprinkle sugar mixture evenly over dough, leaving a ½-inch border. Beginning with a long side, roll up dough jelly-roll fashion; pinch seam to seal (do not seal ends of roll). Cut roll into 15 slices (approximately 1 inch wide). Arrange slices, cut sides up, in prepared pan. Lightly coat rolls with cooking spray; cover and let rise in a warm place (85°), free from drafts, 30 minutes or until doubled in size.
7. Preheat oven to 350°.
8. Uncover rolls, and bake at 350° for 20 minutes or until lightly browned. Let stand 1 minute; carefully invert onto a serving platter. **Yield:** 15 servings (serving size: 1 roll).

CALORIES 275; FAT 7.6g (sat 3.8g, mono 2.6g, poly 0.8g); PROTEIN 4.9g; CARB 47g; FIBER 1.4g; CHOL 15mg; IRON 2.2mg; SODIUM 146mg; CALC 37mg

a little more…

Pairing this with an 8-ounce cup of cappuccino made with fat-free milk will add 50 calories to your meal.

nutrition note

Egg Substitute

Made from egg whites, corn oil, water, flavorings, and preservatives, egg substitute is nutritionally the same as egg whites. If you'd rather use egg whites, replace ¼ cup of egg substitute with two egg whites.

Cardamom-Lime Sweet Rolls

260 calories

1 package dry yeast (about 2¼ teaspoons)
¼ cup warm water (100° to 110°)
½ cup reduced-fat sour cream
⅓ cup granulated sugar
¼ cup butter, melted
1 teaspoon vanilla extract
¾ teaspoon salt
1 large egg, lightly beaten
10.5 ounces all-purpose flour (about 2⅓ cups), divided
   Cooking spray
½ cup packed brown sugar
1 tablespoon grated lime rind
½ to ¾ teaspoon ground cardamom
2 tablespoons butter, melted and divided
1 cup powdered sugar
3 tablespoons fresh lime juice

1. Dissolve yeast in warm water in a small bowl; let stand 5 minutes.
2. Combine sour cream and next 5 ingredients in a large bowl, stirring until well blended. Gradually stir yeast mixture into sour cream mixture. Weigh or lightly spoon flour into dry measuring cups; level with a knife. Add 9 ounces flour (about 2 cups) to sour cream mixture, stirring to form a soft dough.
3. Turn dough out onto a lightly floured surface. Knead until smooth and elastic (about 8 minutes); add enough of remaining 1.5 ounces flour (about ⅓ cup), 1 tablespoon at a time, to prevent dough from sticking to hands (dough will feel slightly tacky).

4. Place dough in a large bowl coated with cooking spray, turning to coat top. Cover and let rise in a warm place (85°), free from drafts, 1 hour or until doubled in size. (Gently press two fingers into dough. If indentation remains, dough has risen enough.)
5. Combine brown sugar, rind, and cardamom. Divide dough into 2 equal portions. Working with 1 portion at a time, roll dough into a 12 x 10–inch rectangle; brush with 1 tablespoon butter. Sprinkle half of filling over dough. Beginning with a long side, roll up jelly-roll fashion; pinch seam to seal (do not seal ends of roll). Repeat procedure with remaining dough, 1 tablespoon butter, and filling. Cut each roll into 12 (1-inch) slices. Place slices, cut sides up, in a 13 x 9–inch baking pan coated with cooking spray. Cover and let rise 30 minutes or until doubled in size.
6. Preheat oven to 350°.
7. Uncover dough. Bake at 350° for 25 minutes or until lightly browned. Cool in pan 5 minutes on a wire rack.
8. To prepare glaze, combine powdered sugar and juice, stirring until smooth. Drizzle glaze over warm rolls. **Yield:** 24 rolls (serving size: 2 rolls).

CALORIES 260; FAT 7.6g (sat 4.6g, mono 1.6g, poly 0.4g); PROTEIN 3.8g; CARB 44.4g; FIBER 1g; CHOL 38mg; IRON 1.6mg; SODIUM 204mg; CALC 34mg

a little more...

Add thick-cut bacon for a salty side. Two pieces will add about 100 calories to your meal.

nutrition note

Cardamom

Cardamom is best stored in whole pod form. Its essential oils are volatile, so the flavor of ground cardamom dissipates quickly. The best pods will be pale sage green with sticky black seeds inside. They're intensely aromatic and have a unique spicy-sweet flavor. Bruise whole pods before using them to allow the flavor to escape. Ten pods equal about 1½ teaspoons ground cardamom.

Blueberry Coffee Cake

This moist, tender blueberry coffee cake scored high in our Test Kitchens, where tasters unanimously considered it a delicious way to use the first blueberries of the season. Studded with plump, juicy pockets of berries, the cake also features a sprinkling of turbinado sugar on top that adds another dimension of texture. Ideal for breakfast, brunch, dessert, or as a snack to savor with coffee, it's a recipe you'll make more than once.

6.75 ounces all-purpose flour (about 1½ cups)
1 teaspoon baking powder
¼ teaspoon baking soda
¼ teaspoon salt
¾ cup granulated sugar
6 tablespoons butter, softened
1 teaspoon vanilla extract
1 large egg
1 large egg white
1⅓ cups low-fat (1%) buttermilk
Cooking spray
2 cups fresh blueberries
1 tablespoon turbinado sugar

1. Preheat oven to 350°.
2. Weigh or lightly spoon flour into dry measuring cups; level with a knife. Combine flour, baking powder, soda, and salt, stirring with a whisk.
3. Place granulated sugar and butter in a large bowl; beat with a mixer at medium speed until well blended (about 2 minutes). Add vanilla, egg, and egg white; beat well. Add flour mixture and buttermilk alternately to sugar mixture, beginning and ending with flour mixture; mix after each addition.

4. Spoon half of batter into a 9-inch round baking pan coated with cooking spray. Sprinkle evenly with 1 cup blueberries. Spoon remaining batter over blueberries; sprinkle evenly with remaining 1 cup blueberries. Sprinkle the top evenly with 1 tablespoon turbinado sugar. Bake at 350° for 50 minutes or until a wooden pick inserted in center comes out clean. Cool in pan 10 minutes on a wire rack; remove from pan. Cool completely on wire rack. Cut into 8 wedges. **Yield:** 8 servings (serving size: 1 wedge).
Note: If using peak-season fruit, use 1½ cups blueberries instead of 2 cups, and only 1 cup buttermilk instead of 1⅓ cups. This will make the batter thicker so the berries won't sink to the bottom.

CALORIES 287; FAT 9.9g (sat 5.9g, mono 2.6g, poly 0.6g); PROTEIN 5.4g; CARB 45.4g; FIBER 1.5g; CHOL 51mg; IRON 1.4mg; SODIUM 294mg; CALC 93mg

a little more...

Serve this sweet coffee cake with a side of turkey breakfast sausage for a savory contrast that also provides filling protein. A 3-ounce serving contains 134 calories and 15 grams of protein.

nutrition note

Regular vs. Low-Fat (1%) Buttermilk

Substituting low-fat buttermilk for regular in your baked goods can have a noticeable impact. In this recipe, making that switch saved 70 calories and 4.9 grams of saturated fat.

Oatmeal with Apples, Hazelnuts, and Flaxseed

If your market sells hazelnuts with the skins removed, you can skip steps 1 and 2, and just finely chop the nuts.

¼ **cup hazelnuts**
3 **cups fat-free milk**
1½ **cups regular oats**
1½ **cups diced Granny Smith apple (about 1 medium)**
⅓ **cup ground flaxseed**
½ **teaspoon ground cinnamon**
¼ **teaspoon salt**
½ **teaspoon vanilla extract**
3 **tablespoons brown sugar**
3 **tablespoons slivered almonds**

1. Preheat oven to 350°.
2. Place hazelnuts on a baking sheet. Bake at 350° for 15 minutes, stirring once. Turn nuts out onto a towel. Roll up towel; rub off skins. Finely chop nuts, and set aside.

3. Combine milk and next 5 ingredients in a medium saucepan. Bring to a boil over medium heat. Stir in vanilla. Cover, reduce heat, and simmer 5 minutes or until thick. Sprinkle with hazelnuts, brown sugar, and almonds. **Yield:** 6 servings (serving size: ⅔ cup).

CALORIES 258; FAT 8.4g (sat 0.9g, mono 4.1g, poly 2.9g); PROTEIN 9.8g; CARB 36.3g; FIBER 6g; CHOL 2mg; IRON 1.9mg; SODIUM 156mg; CALC 203mg

a little more...

Pour a bigger portion of this hot, filling meal. A 1-cup serving contains 387 calories.

nutrition note

Oats

Regular (rolled) oats are made of whole groats that have been steamed and then flattened by large rollers. They're ready in about five minutes and provide a variety of health benefits, including a dose of fiber (1.9 grams in just a ¼-cup serving) that is great for your heart and your digestive tract.

Three-Grain Breakfast Cereal with Walnuts and Dried Fruit

This mixture of barley and oats with nuts and raisins will keep you energized all morning. Walnuts provide omega-3 fatty acids, but pecans also work nicely in this high-fiber cereal. Serve this breakfast cereal with 6 ounces of fat-free yogurt (100 calories) and ¼ cup of sliced fresh strawberries (15 calories) for a complete meal.

½ cup maple syrup
⅓ cup honey
3 tablespoons canola oil
1½ tablespoons vanilla extract
4½ cups regular oats
1 cup uncooked quick-cooking barley
¾ cup chopped walnuts or pecans
½ cup wheat germ
1 teaspoon ground cinnamon
¼ teaspoon ground nutmeg
Cooking spray
1 (7-ounce) package dried mixed fruit (such as Sun-Maid), chopped

1. Preheat oven to 325°.
2. Combine first 4 ingredients, stirring with a whisk.
3. Combine oats and next 5 ingredients in a large bowl. Add syrup mixture; stir well to coat. Spread oat mixture evenly onto a jelly-roll pan coated with cooking spray. Bake at 325° for 30 minutes or until browned, stirring every 10 minutes. Stir in dried fruit. Cool completely.

Yield: 8 cups (serving size: ⅓ cup).

Note: Store in an airtight container for up to 5 days.

CALORIES 185; FAT 5.8g (sat 0.6g, mono 1.7g, poly 2.8g); PROTEIN 4.5g; CARB 31.3g; FIBER 4g; CHOL 0mg; IRON 1.6mg; SODIUM 4mg; CALC 24mg

a little more...

Use a ½-cup serving of this cereal over fat-free yogurt instead of ⅓ cup for an additional 93 calories.

back on track

Use the Scale

Getting on the scale may not be your favorite morning activity, but regular weigh-ins can help you stay on track (or get back on track). If you've fallen off the healthy-eating wagon, the best way to get back on is to face the music and weigh yourself. Don't beat yourself up if you've gained a few pounds. Instead, refocus your efforts, recommit to your healthy lifestyle, and then follow up with weekly weigh-ins to check your progress. If you're trying to lose weight, keep a written record of your weight loss so that even if you've hit a plateau or stumbling block, you can get encouragement and maintain your motivation by seeing your long-term progress.

Lumberjack Hash

Frozen hash browns make this version of the popular diner dish quick and easy.

2 teaspoons vegetable oil
2 teaspoons butter
1 cup chopped onion
1 cup chopped green bell pepper
2 garlic cloves, minced
8 cups frozen shredded hash brown potatoes (about 1 pound), thawed
4 ounces 33%-less-sodium ham, diced
½ teaspoon salt
½ teaspoon black pepper
¾ cup (3 ounces) reduced-fat shredded cheddar cheese

1. Heat oil and butter in a large nonstick skillet over medium heat. Add onion; cook 5 minutes. Add bell pepper and garlic; cook 3 minutes. Add potatoes and next 3 ingredients; cook 16 minutes or until potatoes are golden brown, stirring occasionally. Top with cheese; cook 2 minutes or until cheese melts. **Yield:** 4 servings (serving size: 1¼ cups).

CALORIES 276; FAT 9.1g (sat 4.2g, mono 1.6g, poly 1.6g); PROTEIN 16.5g; CARB 33.7g; FIBER 3.5g; CHOL 33mg; IRON 0.8mg; SODIUM 738mg; CALC 208mg

a little more...

Serve this hearty meal with a fruit salad. A mix of ½ cup of fresh orange sections and ½ cup of grapefruit sections would provide an additional 80 calories plus a dose of vitamin C.

nutrition note

Frozen Hash Browns

When buying frozen hash browns at the grocery store, make sure you choose a plain variety that doesn't contain added seasonings and salt. Read the label. The sodium should be 5 milligrams or less per serving. By choosing an unseasoned variety, you control both the flavor of the dish and the amount of sodium you're consuming.

Jalapeño, Sausage, Jack, and Egg Breakfast Braid

246 calories

1 (13.8-ounce) can refrigerated pizza crust dough
Cooking spray
1 tablespoon olive oil
¼ cup chopped onion
4 ounces chicken sausage with jalapeño peppers, chopped
2 large eggs, lightly beaten
½ cup (2 ounces) shredded Monterey Jack cheese
¼ cup shredded cheddar cheese
¼ cup chopped seeded jalapeño pepper
1 large egg white, lightly beaten

1. Preheat oven to 425°.
2. Unroll dough onto a baking sheet coated with cooking spray; pat into a 15 x 10–inch rectangle.
3. Heat oil in a large skillet over medium heat. Add onion and sausage; cook 9 minutes or until lightly browned. Stir in eggs; cook 1½ minutes or until set. Remove from heat.

4. Sprinkle Monterey Jack lengthwise down center of dough, leaving about a 2½-inch border on each side. Spoon egg mixture evenly over cheese. Sprinkle cheddar over egg mixture; top with jalapeño pepper.
5. Make 2-inch-long diagonal cuts about 1 inch apart on both sides of dough to within ½ inch of filling using a sharp knife or kitchen shears. Arrange strips over filling, alternating strips diagonally over filling. Press ends under to seal. Brush with egg white. Bake at 425° for 15 minutes or until golden brown. Let stand 5 minutes. Cut crosswise into 8 slices. **Yield:** 4 servings (serving size: 2 slices).

CALORIES 246; FAT 15.6g (sat 6.3g, mono 6.6g, poly 1.5g); PROTEIN 15.9g; CARB 11g; FIBER 0.2g; CHOL 147mg; IRON 1.2mg; SODIUM 516mg; CALC 173mg

a little more...

Sweet and savory make a good flavor combination for breakfast, so pair this with 1 cup of grapes (120 calories) to round out this breakfast meal.

nutrition note

Chicken Sausage

When compared to pork sausage, chicken sausage offers a substantial nutritional savings. By choosing chicken, you can save about 50 calories and 2.5 grams of saturated fat per 2-ounce serving.

Simple Baked Eggs

This is the easiest way to prepare and serve several individual portions. Serve it with a slice of whole-wheat toast (80 calories) and an orange (80 calories) to complete the meal.

1   tablespoon butter
6   large eggs
1   teaspoon freshly ground black pepper
¾   teaspoon salt
2   tablespoons whipping cream

1. Preheat oven to 350°.
2. Coat each of 6 (6-ounce) ramekins or custard cups with ½ teaspoon butter. Break 1 egg into each prepared ramekin. Sprinkle eggs evenly with pepper and salt; spoon 1 teaspoon cream over each egg. Place ramekins in a 13 x 9–inch baking dish; add hot water to pan to a depth of 1¼ inches. Bake at 350° for 25 minutes or until eggs are set. **Yield:** 6 servings (serving size: 1 egg).

CALORIES 109; FAT 8.7g (sat 3.9g, mono 2.9g, poly 0.8g); PROTEIN 6.5g; CARB 0.8g; FIBER 0.1g; CHOL 223mg; IRON 0.9mg; SODIUM 380mg; CALC 32mg

a little more...

Add a second piece of whole-wheat toast and top them with 1 tablespoon of jam or jelly. These additions will add 130 calories to your meal.

quick fix

Snow Days

While snowy winters may keep some inside, it can be an ideal time to experience winter sports that can keep you in shape and energized. Get outside for 30 minutes of cross-country skiing (you'll burn more than 300 calories), snowshoeing (more than 250 calories), or sledding (more than 200 calories).

Whispery Eggs with Crabmeat and Herbs

222 calories

Whisking the eggs vigorously (even with an immersion blender) yields fluffy, whispery results.

4 large eggs, lightly beaten
2 large egg whites, lightly beaten
1 tablespoon crème fraîche
¼ teaspoon fine sea salt
¼ teaspoon freshly ground black pepper
1 teaspoon butter
1 teaspoon olive oil
1 shallot, thinly sliced
4 teaspoons chopped fresh parsley
1 teaspoon chopped fresh tarragon
1 teaspoon chopped fresh thyme
1 cup lump crabmeat, drained and shell pieces removed
16 (½-inch-thick) slices diagonally cut French bread baguette, toasted
   Thyme sprigs (optional)
   Louisiana hot sauce (optional)

1. Combine eggs and egg whites in a large bowl; beat vigorously with a whisk 1 minute. Add crème fraîche, salt, and pepper; beat vigorously with a whisk 1 minute.

2. Heat butter and oil in a large non-stick skillet over medium-high heat. Add shallots to pan; sauté 2 minutes, stirring frequently. Stir in parsley, tarragon, and thyme. Reduce heat to medium-low. Whisk egg mixture. Add egg mixture to pan; cook 1 minute, stirring occasionally. Fold in crabmeat; cook 1 minute or until eggs reach desired consistency, stirring gently. Arrange 4 baguette slices on each of 4 plates; spoon 1 cup egg mixture onto each serving. Garnish with thyme sprigs and serve with hot sauce, if desired. **Yield:** 4 servings.

CALORIES 222; FAT 8.9g (sat 3.2g, mono 3.5g, poly 1.1g); PROTEIN 16.9g; CARB 18.9g; FIBER 0.7g; CHOL 247mg; IRON 2.3mg; SODIUM 517mg; CALC 65mg

a little more...

Pair this brunch-worthy meal with a glass of wine. A fuller-bodied, rich rosé sparkler will complement both the crabmeat and the protein of the eggs—a 5-ounce pour will add 100 calories.

back on track

Schedule Something New

If your motivation is lagging, consider buying a package of sessions with a personal trainer or sign up for a new group workout class, and schedule your appointments now. It can infuse new life into your workouts, and you won't want to waste workout sessions that you've already paid for.

Scrambled Eggs with Morel and Tarragon Cream Sauce

295 calories

Soft-scrambling the eggs prevents them from drying out and keeps them tender—cook slowly over medium heat, and stir them to a custard-like texture. For brunch, serve this dish with a quick toss-together salad (1 cup spinach, ¼ cup cherry tomatoes, and 1 tablespoon fat-free balsamic vinaigrette per serving) for an additional 30 calories. Or pair with fruit for breakfast.

½ cup (about ½ ounce) dried morel mushrooms
2 teaspoons butter
¼ cup finely chopped shallots
½ cup organic vegetable broth
1 teaspoon fresh lemon juice
⅓ cup reduced-fat sour cream
2 teaspoons chopped fresh chives, divided
2 teaspoons chopped fresh tarragon, divided
½ teaspoon salt, divided
¼ teaspoon freshly ground black pepper, divided
Cooking spray
3 large eggs
3 large egg whites
4 English muffins, split and toasted
Tarragon leaves (optional)

1. Place mushrooms in a bowl, and cover with boiling water. Cover and let stand 20 minutes or until tender. Drain well; coarsely chop.
2. Melt butter in a large nonstick skillet over medium-high heat. Add shallots; sauté 1 minute. Add mushrooms; sauté 2 minutes. Add broth and juice; cook 2 minutes. Remove from heat; stir in sour cream. Stir in 1 teaspoon chives, 1 teaspoon tarragon, ¼ teaspoon salt, and ⅛ teaspoon pepper. Place mushroom sauce in a small bowl; cover and keep warm. Wipe pan clean with a paper towel.
3. Heat pan over medium heat, and coat with cooking spray. Whisk together remaining 1 teaspoon chives, 1 teaspoon tarragon, ¼ teaspoon salt, ⅛ teaspoon black pepper, eggs, and egg whites. Pour egg mixture into pan. Cook 4 minutes or until soft-scrambled, stirring frequently.
4. Place 2 muffin halves, cut sides up, on each of 4 plates. Top each serving with about 3 tablespoons sauce and ¼ cup eggs. Garnish with tarragon leaves, if desired. **Yield:** 4 servings.

CALORIES 265; FAT 9.2g (sat 4.1g, mono 2.9g, poly 1.2g); PROTEIN 14.3g; CARB 31.6g; FIBER 1.8g; CHOL 171mg; IRON 3.4mg; SODIUM 732mg; CALC 152mg

a little more...

Add a glass of apple juice to this meal. A 1-cup serving will add 115 calories.

nutrition note

Eggs and Cholesterol

Eggs do have a place in a healthy diet. For years, the much-maligned egg received a bad nutritional grade because of its cholesterol content, but in this instance, moderation is key. Along with cholesterol, eggs contain a variety of good-for-you vitamins (vitamins A, B₁₂, and E), minerals (iron, selenium, and trace amounts of calcium), and antioxidants, plus a dose of protein (more than 6 grams per egg).

Eggs Benedict Florentine with Creamy Butter Sauce

264 calories

- 1 tablespoon cornstarch
- ½ cup water
- ⅓ cup low-fat buttermilk
- 2 large eggs
- 2 tablespoons Clarified Butter
- ½ teaspoon salt
- Cooking spray
- ½ teaspoon minced garlic
- ¼ teaspoon salt
- ¼ teaspoon freshly ground black pepper
- 6 large egg whites
- 4 large eggs
- 6 cups fresh spinach, trimmed
- 8 English muffins, split and toasted
- 8 (½-ounce) slices Canadian bacon, each cut in half
- 3 tablespoons chopped fresh chives
- ¼ teaspoon freshly ground black pepper

1. Place cornstarch in the top of a double boiler. Combine ½ cup water, buttermilk, and 2 eggs, stirring well with a whisk. Add egg mixture to cornstarch; stir well. Cook over simmering water until thick and mixture reaches 160° (about 7 minutes), stirring constantly. Stir in Clarified Butter and ½ teaspoon salt. Remove from heat. Cover and keep warm.

2. Heat a nonstick skillet over medium heat. Coat pan with cooking spray. Add garlic to pan; cook 30 seconds, stirring frequently. Combine ¼ teaspoon salt, pepper, egg whites, and 4 eggs, stirring well with a whisk. Add egg mixture to pan; cook 5 minutes or until set, stirring occasionally.

3. Place spinach in a large nonstick skillet over medium-high heat; cook 4 minutes or just until slightly wilted, stirring frequently. Place 2 muffin halves, cut sides up, on each of 8 plates. Place half a Canadian bacon slice on each muffin half, and top each serving with about ¼ cup spinach. Place about ¼ cup egg mixture on each serving, and top each serving with about 2 tablespoons sauce. Sprinkle evenly with chopped fresh chives and ¼ teaspoon pepper. Serve immediately. **Yield:** 8 servings. **Note:** Nutritional analysis includes Clarified Butter.

CALORIES 264; FAT 8.8g (sat 3.6g, mono 3g, poly 1.2g); PROTEIN 16.4g; CARB 29.9g; FIBER 0.4g; CHOL 174mg; IRON 3.7mg; SODIUM 714mg; CALC 155mg

Clarified Butter

- ½ cup unsalted butter

1. Place butter in a saucepan over medium-low heat; cook 5 minutes or until completely melted. Skim solids off top with a spoon; discard solids. Slowly pour remaining butter out of pan, leaving remaining solids in pan; discard solids. **Yield:** about ⅓ cup (serving size: 1 teaspoon).

CALORIES 37; FAT 4g (sat 2.6g, mono 1.2g, poly 0.2g); PROTEIN 0g; CARB 0g; FIBER 0g; CHOL 11mg; IRON 0mg; SODIUM 0mg; CALC 0mg

a little more...

Serve with a glass of orange juice. It'll add 110 calories to the meal.

quick fix

Tennis

After breakfast, grab your tennis racket and a friend for a tennis match. You'll burn about 250 calories during a 30-minute game.

Herb and Goat Cheese Omelet

233 calories

A tender omelet gains a salty boost from goat cheese without adding too much sodium.

4 large eggs
1 tablespoon water
¼ teaspoon freshly ground black pepper, divided
⅛ teaspoon salt
¼ cup (1 ounce) crumbled goat cheese
1 teaspoon chopped fresh parsley
½ teaspoon chopped fresh tarragon
2 teaspoons olive oil, divided
½ cup thinly sliced zucchini
½ cup (3 x ¼–inch) julienne-cut red bell pepper
Dash of salt
1 teaspoon chopped fresh chives

1. Combine eggs and 1 tablespoon water in a bowl, stirring with a whisk. Stir in ⅛ teaspoon black pepper and ⅛ teaspoon salt. Combine goat cheese, parsley, and tarragon in a small bowl.
2. Heat 1 teaspoon olive oil in an 8-inch nonstick skillet over medium heat. Add remaining ⅛ teaspoon black pepper, zucchini, bell pepper, and dash of salt to pan; cook 4 minutes or until tender. Remove zucchini mixture from pan; cover and keep warm.
3. Place ½ teaspoon oil in pan. Pour half of egg mixture into pan, and let egg mixture set slightly (do not stir). Carefully loosen set edges of omelet with a spatula, tipping pan to pour uncooked egg to sides. Continue this procedure for about 5 seconds or until almost no runny egg remains. Sprinkle half of cheese mixture evenly over omelet; cook omelet 1 minute or until set. Slide omelet onto plate, folding into thirds. Repeat procedure with remaining ½ teaspoon oil, egg mixture, and goat cheese mixture. Sprinkle chives over omelets. Serve with zucchini mixture. **Yield:** 2 servings (serving size: 1 omelet and ½ cup vegetables).

CALORIES 233; FAT 17.6g (sat 5.8g, mono 7.8g, poly 2g); PROTEIN 16g; CARB 3.6g; FIBER 1g; CHOL 430mg; IRON 2.5mg; SODIUM 416mg; CALC 84mg

a little more...

Serve with seedy whole-grain toast (80 calories) to complete this hearty meal ideal for brunch.

nutrition note

Substituting Some Salt

Salt provides a precise package of sodium and chloride, minerals that are essential to the electrolyte balance in our bodies. Plus, nothing quite satisfies like salt. But Americans tend to take in too much. The average American consumes 3,600 milligrams of sodium each day—1,300 milligrams above the daily recommendation of 2,300 milligrams. There are other ways to add flavor without too much assistance from the salt shaker. One way is to let small amounts of salty, high-sodium ingredients shine. For example, just a little grated or finely shredded full-flavored cheese adds a punch of indulgent flavor without adding excessive sodium.

Summer Vegetable Frittata

Fresh seasonal produce enhances the flavor of this Italian omelet.

1½	**tablespoons olive oil**
1	**cup diced zucchini**
½	**cup chopped red bell pepper**
⅓	**cup chopped onion**
1	**tablespoon chopped fresh thyme**
½	**teaspoon salt, divided**
¼	**teaspoon freshly ground black pepper, divided**
2	**garlic cloves, minced**
½	**cup chopped seeded tomato**
9	**large eggs**

1. Heat olive oil in a 10-inch broilerproof skillet over medium heat. Add zucchini, bell pepper, onion, thyme, ¼ teaspoon salt, ⅛ teaspoon black pepper, and garlic. Cover and cook 7 minutes or until vegetables are tender, stirring occasionally. Stir in tomato. Cook, uncovered, 5 minutes or until liquid evaporates.

2. Combine eggs, remaining ¼ teaspoon salt, and remaining ⅛ teaspoon black pepper in a medium bowl; stir with a whisk until frothy. Pour egg mixture into pan over vegetables, stirring gently. Cover, reduce heat, and cook 15 minutes or until almost set in center.

3. Preheat broiler.

4. Broil frittata 3 minutes or until set. Invert onto a serving platter; cut into 8 wedges. **Yield:** 4 servings (serving size: 2 wedges).

CALORIES 227; FAT 16.4g (sat 4.2g, mono 8g, poly 2.1g); PROTEIN 15.1g; CARB 5.5g; FIBER 1.1g; CHOL 476mg; IRON 2.4mg; SODIUM 458mg; CALC 80mg

a little more...

Pair this meal with a delicious summer fruit. One cup of fresh peach slices will add 65 calories to this meal.

nutrition note

Tomatoes

Lycopene is the disease-fighting antioxidant behind the bold red color of tomatoes. Studies have found that lycopene—with its ability to protect cells and other structures in the body from oxygen damage—helps prevent heart disease and a variety of cancers.

Breakfast Tortilla

You can substitute pecorino Romano cheese for Manchego. Serve with 2 slices of center-cut bacon, which adds 40 calories to the meal.

½ **pound Yukon gold potato (about 1 medium)**
1 **tablespoon minced fresh chives, divided**
¾ **teaspoon salt, divided**
½ **teaspoon freshly ground black pepper**
4 **large eggs**
1 **large egg white**
1 **tablespoon olive oil**
1 **garlic clove, minced**
3 **tablespoons finely grated Manchego cheese**
1 **teaspoon extra-virgin olive oil**
½ **cup halved grape or cherry tomatoes**
Freshly ground black pepper (optional)

1. Preheat oven to 350°.
2. Place potato in a saucepan; cover with water. Bring to a boil. Reduce heat, and simmer 20 minutes or until tender; drain. Cool. Peel potato; thinly slice.
3. Combine 2 teaspoons chives, ¼ teaspoon salt, pepper, eggs, and egg white in a bowl; stir with a whisk until blended.
4. Heat 1 tablespoon oil in an 8-inch ovenproof nonstick skillet over medium heat. Add garlic and potato slices; cook 30 seconds, gently turning potato to coat with oil. Sprinkle with remaining ½ teaspoon salt. Press potato mixture with a spatula into a solid layer in bottom of pan. Pour egg mixture over potato mixture; cook 1 minute. Gently stir egg and potato mixture. Press potato back down in bottom of pan; cook 2 minutes. Remove from heat. Sprinkle with cheese.
5. Bake at 350° for 7 minutes or until center is set. Remove from oven. Drizzle with 1 teaspoon extra-virgin olive oil. Loosen sides of tortilla from pan, and gently slide onto a serving platter. Top with tomatoes and remaining 1 teaspoon chives. Sprinkle with black pepper, if desired. Cut into 4 wedges. **Yield:** 4 servings (serving size: 1 wedge and 2 tablespoons tomatoes).

CALORIES 190; FAT 10.7g (sat 2.8g, mono 5.5g, poly 1.2g); PROTEIN 10g; CARB 14g; FIBER 1.2g; CHOL 215mg; IRON 1.3mg; SODIUM 581mg; CALC 77mg

a little more...

For a more substantial meal, serve 2 wedges of Breakfast Tortilla.

nutrition note

Manchego Cheese

This cheese is made in the La Mancha region of Spain from Manchega sheep's milk. Nutritionally, sheep's milk cheese is slightly higher in fat than cheese made from cow's milk, creating a rich, creamy cheese. And like most cheese, it provides a dose of bone-strengthening calcium.

Quick Breakfast Burritos

This recipe yields an easy, satisfying breakfast. Add more ground red pepper if you like your food hot and spicy. Serve with a cup of a mix of fresh pineapple, strawberries, and kiwifruit, which will add 80 calories to this meal.

PICO DE GALLO
- 1½ cups chopped tomato (about 1 large)
- ½ cup chopped green onions
- ½ cup chopped fresh cilantro
- 2 teaspoons fresh lemon juice
- ⅛ teaspoon salt
- ⅛ teaspoon black pepper
- Dash of crushed red pepper

BURRITOS
- ¼ teaspoon chopped fresh oregano
- ⅛ teaspoon salt
- ⅛ teaspoon black pepper
- 4 eggs, lightly beaten
- Dash of ground red pepper
- Cooking spray
- ¼ cup chopped onion
- 1 (2-ounce) can diced green chiles
- 4 (6-inch) corn tortillas
- ½ cup (2 ounces) shredded colby-Jack cheese

1. To prepare pico de gallo, combine first 7 ingredients in a small bowl.

2. To prepare burritos, combine oregano and next 4 ingredients in a small bowl, stirring well with a whisk.

3. Heat a large nonstick skillet over medium heat. Coat pan with cooking spray. Add egg mixture, chopped onion, and green chiles to pan. Cook 3 minutes or until eggs are set, stirring frequently. Remove pan from heat; stir egg mixture well.

4. Heat corn tortillas according to package directions. Divide egg mixture evenly among tortillas. Top each serving with 2 tablespoons cheese and about ⅓ cup pico de gallo. **Yield:** 4 servings (serving size: 1 burrito).

CALORIES 197; FAT 10.8g (sat 4.5g, mono 3.5g, poly 1.2g); PROTEIN 12.7g; CARB 14.3g; FIBER 2.4g; CHOL 258mg; IRON 1.7mg; SODIUM 372mg; CALC 170mg

a little more...

Serve this savory breakfast with 1 cup of 1% low-fat chocolate milk. You'll add about 160 calories to this meal, but get 288 milligrams of calcium—more than one-fourth of the daily recommendation.

back on track

Think Before You Drink

Pour chocolate milk into two glasses of equal volume: One short and wide, the other tall and thin. Most people pour 19 percent more in the short glass because the eye is a poor judge of volume in relation to height and width. Your best bet: Measure your drink serving for caloric beverages until you get used to a proper serving in your glassware.

Sausage and Cheese Breakfast Casserole

Prep this the night before for an easy breakfast or brunch. Find turkey sausage in the refrigerated or freezer section of the supermarket with other breakfast meats.

Cooking spray
12 ounces turkey breakfast sausage
2 cups 1% low-fat milk
2 cups egg substitute
1 teaspoon dry mustard
¾ teaspoon salt
½ teaspoon freshly ground black pepper
¼ teaspoon ground red pepper
3 large eggs
16 (1-ounce) slices white bread
1 cup (4 ounces) reduced-fat finely shredded extrasharp cheddar cheese
¼ teaspoon paprika

1. Heat a large nonstick skillet over medium-high heat. Coat pan with cooking spray. Add sausage to pan; cook 5 minutes or until browned, stirring and breaking sausage to crumble. Remove from heat; cool.
2. Combine milk and next 6 ingredients in a large bowl, stirring with a whisk.
3. Trim crusts from bread. Cut bread into 1-inch cubes. Add bread cubes, sausage, and cheddar cheese to milk mixture, stirring to combine. Pour bread mixture into a 13 x 9–inch baking dish or 3-quart casserole dish coated with cooking spray, spreading egg mixture evenly in baking dish. Cover and refrigerate 8 hours or overnight.
4. Preheat oven to 350°.
5. Remove casserole from refrigerator; let stand 30 minutes. Sprinkle casserole evenly with paprika. Bake at 350° for 45 minutes or until set and lightly browned. Let stand 10 minutes. **Yield:** 10 servings (serving size: about 1¼ cups).

CALORIES 221; FAT 8.2g (sat 3.8g, mono 1.8g, poly 1g); PROTEIN 19.1g; CARB 16.8g; FIBER 0.7g; CHOL 91mg; IRON 2.6mg; SODIUM 763mg; CALC 217mg

a little more...

Make this casserole serve 8 with a larger (about 1½ cups) portion. The calories still fall within the breakfast budget at 276 calories per serving. To further fill out the meal, pair it with 1 cup of fresh watermelon, which will add 45 colorful calories.

back on track

Downsize Your Dishes

If you're one of the 54 percent of Americans who eat until their plates are clean, make sure those plates are modestly sized. On a standard 8- to 10-inch plate, a portion of your breakfast casserole looks like a meal. On a 12- to 14-inch plate, it looks meager, so you're likely to dish out a bigger portion to fill the plate.

Three Quick Smoothies

Serve a slice of whole-wheat toast topped with 1 teaspoon of butter as a side for a Peach-Mango Smoothie or Strawberry-Guava Smoothie. This simple addition adds 113 calories to either of these quick meals. In a Banana Breakfast Smoothie, adding the yogurt at the very end imparts a creamy texture to the smoothie.

Peach-Mango Smoothie

297 calories

⅔ cup frozen sliced peaches
⅔ cup frozen mango pieces (such as Dole)
⅔ cup peach nectar
1 tablespoon honey
1 (6-ounce) carton organic peach fat-free yogurt

1. Place all ingredients in a blender; process 2 minutes or until smooth. Serve immediately. **Yield:** 2 servings (serving size: 1 cup).

CALORIES 184; FAT 0.3g (sat 0.1g, mono 0.1g, poly 0.1g); PROTEIN 4.1g; CARB 44g; FIBER 2.4g; CHOL 2mg; IRON 0.4mg; SODIUM 50mg; CALC 107mg

Strawberry-Guava Smoothie

269 calories

1 cup quartered strawberries (about 5 ounces)
½ cup guava nectar
1 (6-ounce) carton organic strawberry fat-free yogurt
1 frozen sliced small ripe banana
5 ice cubes (about 2 ounces)

1. Place all ingredients in a blender; process 2 minutes or until smooth. Serve immediately. **Yield:** 2 servings (serving size: about 1¼ cups).

CALORIES 156; FAT 0.5g (sat 0.1g, mono 0.1g, poly 0.2g); PROTEIN 4.2g; CARB 36.2g; FIBER 3.6g; CHOL 2mg; IRON 0.5mg; SODIUM 49mg; CALC 116mg

Banana Breakfast Smoothie

212 calories

½ cup 1% low-fat milk
½ cup crushed ice
1 tablespoon honey
⅛ teaspoon ground nutmeg
1 frozen sliced large ripe banana
1 cup plain Greek 2% yogurt

1. Place first 5 ingredients in a blender; process 2 minutes or until smooth. Add yogurt; process just until blended. Serve immediately. **Yield:** 2 servings (serving size: 1 cup).

CALORIES 212; FAT 3.6g (sat 2.5g, mono 0.2g, poly 0.1g); PROTEIN 14.2g; CARB 34.2g; FIBER 2g; CHOL 9mg; IRON 0.3mg; SODIUM 75mg; CALC 200mg

a little more...

Substitute the butter on the toast with a tablespoon of natural peanut butter. It adds protein and healthy fats for a quick side (that adds 173 calories to the amount found in the smoothies).

nutrition note

Smoothies

At their core, smoothies are healthy: Fruits, vegetables, and lower-fat dairy, lightly sweetened, and whirred together into a refreshing drink that provides vitamins, minerals, and antioxidants. Sized sensibly, it's an ideal on-the-go breakfast, but supersized smoothies from various smoothie shops can provide way more calories than you bargained for at breakfast—anywhere from 300 to more than 1,000 per serving. Check the nutritional information before you order. Or, better yet, make your own.

Breakfast Parfaits

279 calories

Assemble everything but the granola and almonds ahead of time, and store in the refrigerator for up to an hour. Sprinkle with granola and almonds just before serving for optimum crunch.

⅓ **cup apricot preserves**
3 **cups sliced strawberries**
2 **cups vanilla low-fat yogurt**
½ **cup low-fat granola without raisins (such as Kellogg's)**
2 **tablespoons slivered almonds, toasted**

1. Place apricot preserves in a medium microwave-safe bowl, and microwave at HIGH 10 to 15 seconds or until preserves melt. Add strawberries, and toss gently to coat.
2. Spoon ¼ cup yogurt into each of 4 parfait glasses; top each serving with ⅓ cup strawberry mixture. Repeat layers with remaining yogurt and strawberry mixture. Top each serving with 2 tablespoons granola and 1½ teaspoons almonds. Serve immediately. **Yield:** 4 servings (serving size: 1 parfait).

CALORIES 279; FAT 4.2g (sat 1.4g, mono 1.4g, poly 0.6g); PROTEIN 8.7g; CARB 53.5g; FIBER 3.9g; CHOL 6mg; IRON 1mg; SODIUM 94mg; CALC 240mg

a little more...

Scramble two eggs for a quick way to bulk up this meal. This protein-rich addition provides 140 calories.

nutrition note

Yogurt

Yogurt is an excellent source of calcium. Many brands contain about 40 percent of daily calcium needs based on an 8-ounce serving. (We recommend low-fat and fat-free varieties.) Plus, yogurt is a tasty and versatile food that can be enjoyed for breakfast, or as a snack or dessert.

lunch

- Healthy Ideas for the Middle of the Day
- Eating Out Tips
- Recipes

lunch

For many of us, lunch is a stress-filled hour (or less) spent dealing with traffic and fast-food drive-thru lines. Or there's the ever-popular all-you-can-eat lunch buffet that leaves you wondering how you'll make it to the end of the day without a nap and bursting a button.

But it doesn't have to be this way. Lunch can be a relaxing time in which you go at your own pace and come back to your desk satisfied, both mentally and physically. Resist the call of the drive-thru and the ease of prepackaged, highly processed foods, and instead pack your own. Brown-bagging it allows you to enjoy your midday meal without stress, and it saves you money. Plus, you'll enjoy a more healthful meal—one that's certainly more healthful than the alternatives. But this doesn't mean you're doomed to endless PB&Js or bland, frozen meals. Try these recipes and follow our tips, and the office lounge will become the best place in town for an enjoyable lunch and a true break.

Healthy Ideas for the Middle of the Day

With just a little organization and a few supplies—such as an insulated bag and serving-sized containers—your lunch-box options can be invitingly inspired. Try these tips to ensure brown-bagging success every time.

• **Make dishes ahead when possible.** The flavor of many soups and stews (like Barley and Beef Soup, page 152) and dips, such as hummus, improves with time; make them the night before.

• **Keep it separate.** To prevent soggy sandwiches, pack separate zip-top bags of tomato slices, lettuce, and bread, then assemble the sandwiches just before serving. Similarly, don't dress leafy salads until you are ready to eat. Salt will draw moisture out of watery ingredients, so add items such as tomatoes and cucumbers to a grain salad at the last minute for the best results. However, some sandwiches (like Tuna Pan Bagnat, page 118) are meant to absorb some liquid from the filling, and therefore should be assembled ahead of time.

• **Put leftovers to good use.** Consider applying extras from dinner to the next day's lunch. Slice leftover chicken or beef and serve it on top of pasta or salad greens, mix it into a grain salad (such as Tabbouleh with Chicken and Red Pepper, page 110), or make it into a sandwich. Chop extra grilled vegetables and add them to soups, salads, or sandwiches.

• **Stay safe.** Keep cold food cold (below 40°) and hot food hot (above 140°) as it travels. Use insulated lunch bags, coolers, thermoses, ice bags, and frozen gel packs to help with temperature control. If reheating items in a microwave, the United States Department of Agriculture recommends they reach 165° and are served steaming hot.

Eating Out Tips

With supersized sandwiches and sides as the typical drive-thru fare, keeping to an allotted number of calories for a lunch out can be difficult. In general, choose sandwiches that are filled with lots of fresh produce—they'll add flavor and nutrients for very few calories. You'll want to stick with one slice of cheese (or none at all) for your sandwich and limit the creamy, calorie-rich condiments you add to them (or have them served on the side and use just a little). Also, skip the fried sides and opt for fruit or salads topped with light dressings (oil and vinegar–based dressings are generally lower in calories and fat than creamy dressings). And always practice portion control. Those hefty sandwiches mean the calories are hefty, too.

• *A 6-inch Subway Club on wheat (without cheese) from Subway* = 320 calories
• *Half of a Napa Almond Chicken Salad Sandwich on Sesame Semolina with a fruit cup (watermelon and strawberries) from Panera* = 400 calories
• *A Premium Grilled Chicken Classic Sandwich from McDonald's* = 420 calories

Taco Rice Salad

360 calories

Convenience products, such as preseasoned yellow rice and picante sauce, flavor this easy one-dish meal that appeals to kids and adults alike.

SALAD

Cooking spray
- 1 pound ground round
- 1 garlic clove, minced
- 3 cups cooked yellow rice
- 1 teaspoon ground cumin
- 1 teaspoon chili powder
- ¼ teaspoon salt
- ¼ teaspoon black pepper
- 6 cups torn romaine lettuce (about 10 ounces)
- 3 cups chopped tomato (about 1¼ pounds)
- 1 cup frozen whole-kernel corn, thawed
- ½ cup chopped red onion
- 1 (15-ounce) can black beans, rinsed and drained

DRESSING
- ⅔ cup fat-free sour cream
- ⅔ cup picante sauce
- 1 teaspoon chili powder
- ½ teaspoon ground cumin

REMAINING INGREDIENT
- ½ cup (2 ounces) reduced-fat shredded sharp cheddar cheese

1. To prepare salad, heat a large nonstick skillet over medium-high heat. Coat pan with cooking spray. Add beef and garlic, and cook 9 minutes or until browned, stirring to crumble. Drain; return beef mixture to pan. Stir in rice and next 4 ingredients. Cool slightly.

2. Combine lettuce and next 4 ingredients in a large bowl; toss to combine.

3. To prepare dressing, combine sour cream, picante sauce, 1 teaspoon chili powder, and ½ teaspoon cumin, stirring with a whisk. Spoon dressing over lettuce mixture; toss to coat. Place 1⅓ cups lettuce mixture on each of 6 plates. Top with ¾ cup rice mixture and about 1½ tablespoons cheese. **Yield:** 6 servings.

CALORIES 360; FAT 11.9g (sat 5g, mono 4.5g, poly 0.8g); PROTEIN 21.1g; CARB 46.7g; FIBER 6.7g; CHOL 48mg; IRON 4.2mg; SODIUM 994mg; CALC 177mg

a little more...

Serve with 1 ounce of light baked tortilla chips. They'll add 134 calories to your meal.

nutrition note

Ground Round

When buying ground beef, look at the percentages. Ground round is 15 percent fat, while ground chuck is slightly higher at 20 percent fat and ground sirloin is leaner with 10 percent fat. You might also find ground beef at your grocery store simply labeled "lean ground beef" with 7 percent fat. You can substitute a leaner ground beef in this recipe if you like—just realize that with less fat, the taste may be altered slightly.

Shrimp Caesar Salad

Precooked shrimp speed up preparation. If you purchase raw shrimp, cook them in boiling water for 2 minutes or until done. Sriracha adds spicy heat to the dressing; omit it if you'd prefer a milder dish. Serve with a 1-ounce baguette slice (75 calories) to complete the meal.

DRESSING
- 2 tablespoons light mayonnaise
- 2 tablespoons water
- 2 tablespoons fresh lemon juice
- 1 teaspoon grated Parmesan cheese
- ¼ teaspoon freshly ground black pepper
- ¼ teaspoon Sriracha (hot chile sauce, such as Huy Fong)
- ⅛ teaspoon Worcestershire sauce
- 2 garlic cloves, minced

SALAD
- 1½ pounds medium shrimp, cooked, peeled, and deveined
- ¾ cup fat-free seasoned croutons
- 2 tablespoons grated Parmesan cheese
- 1 (10-ounce) package chopped romaine lettuce
- 3 tablespoons pine nuts, toasted
- Chopped fresh chives (optional)

1. To prepare dressing, combine first 8 ingredients, stirring with a whisk.
2. To prepare salad, combine shrimp and next 3 ingredients in a large bowl. Add dressing; toss well to coat. Top with pine nuts. Garnish with chives, if desired. Serve immediately. **Yield:** 4 servings (serving size: 3 cups salad and 2¼ teaspoons pine nuts).

CALORIES 295; FAT 9.4g (sat 1.7g, mono 2.1g, poly 4g); PROTEIN 38.6g; CARB 12.2g; FIBER 1.8g; CHOL 261mg; IRON 5.2mg; SODIUM 462mg; CALC 149mg

a little more...

For a weekend lunch, pair this with a 5-ounce glass of sauvignon blanc. It'll add 116 calories.

nutrition note

Shellfish and Cholesterol

While some shellfish, including shrimp and lobster, are high in cholesterol, that doesn't mean you shouldn't enjoy them. Cholesterol found in food has little effect on the cholesterol levels of most people. The primary culprits known to increase cholesterol are saturated fats and trans fats, both of which are low or nonexistent in shellfish.

BLT Bread Salad

Think of this hearty tossed salad as a deconstructed BLT sandwich, where the bread appears in the form of croutons. Round out the plate with a couple slices of fresh cantaloupe, which provide 47 calories.

6	ounces French bread baguette, cut into ½-inch cubes
	Cooking spray
4	slices hickory-smoked bacon
1	tablespoon olive oil
¼	cup red wine vinegar
¼	teaspoon freshly ground black pepper
⅛	teaspoon salt
6	cups torn romaine lettuce
1½	pounds plum tomatoes, cut into ½-inch wedges
3	green onions, thinly sliced
½	cup (2 ounces) crumbled feta cheese

1. Preheat oven to 350°.
2. Layer bread on a baking sheet; coat with cooking spray. Bake at 350° for 18 minutes or until toasted.
3. Cook bacon in a large nonstick skillet over medium heat until crisp. Remove bacon from pan, reserving 1 tablespoon drippings in pan. Cut bacon into ½-inch pieces. Stir oil into bacon drippings in pan; remove from heat. Stir in vinegar, pepper, and salt.
4. Combine lettuce, tomatoes, and onions in a large bowl; drizzle with vinaigrette. Add bread; toss well to coat. Sprinkle with bacon and cheese. Serve immediately.
Yield: 4 servings (serving size: about 2 cups).

CALORIES 315; FAT 14.4g (sat 6g, mono 6.4g, poly 1.6g); PROTEIN 10.5g; CARB 37.6g; FIBER 4.7g; CHOL 26mg; IRON 3.3mg; SODIUM 788mg; CALC 116mg

a little more...

Stir in ½ cup of chopped cooked chicken breast per serving for a heartier meal. This protein-rich addition will add 116 calories.

nutrition note

Spectacular Salads

Salads are an excellent way to get your greens in as well as an assortment of vitamins, minerals, fiber, and antioxidants, but that doesn't mean they have to be boring. The key is adding small amounts of some higher-fat (but highly satisfying) ingredients, such as crumbled bacon and cheese as we have in this recipe. They'll add loads of savory flavor without adding too many calories.

Peppery Monterey Jack Pasta Salad

371 calories

Acini di pepe [ah-CHEE-nee dee-PAY-pay] are tiny pasta rounds resembling peppercorns. Use ditalini (very short tube-shaped macaroni) or any other small pasta shape if you can't find acini di pepe in your supermarket.

- 6 ounces uncooked acini di pepe pasta (about 1 cup)
- 2¼ cups diced plum tomato (about 14 ounces)
- ⅓ cup capers, rinsed and drained
- ¼ cup finely chopped red onion
- ¼ cup sliced pickled banana peppers
- ¼ cup chopped fresh parsley
- 2 tablespoons cider vinegar
- 1 tablespoon extra-virgin olive oil
- ½ teaspoon dried oregano
- ⅛ teaspoon salt
- 2 ounces Monterey Jack cheese, cut into ¼-inch cubes
- 1 (16-ounce) can navy beans, rinsed and drained
- 1 ounce salami, chopped
- 1 garlic clove, minced

1. Cook pasta according to package directions, omitting salt and fat. Drain.
2. Combine tomato and next 12 ingredients in a large bowl. Add pasta to tomato mixture, tossing well to combine. **Yield:** 4 servings (serving size: about 1½ cups).

CALORIES 371; FAT 11.6g (sat 4.7g, mono 5.3g, poly 1.4g); PROTEIN 16.6g; CARB 51.7g; FIBER 6.3g; CHOL 21mg; IRON 3.5mg; SODIUM 919mg; CALC 164mg

a little more...

Serve with Asiago Breadsticks for an additional 99 calories per breadstick.

Asiago Breadsticks

Freeze leftover baked breadsticks, completely cooled and tightly wrapped, for up to one month.

- ½ cup grated Asiago cheese
- 1 tablespoon sesame seeds
- 1 teaspoon freshly ground black pepper
- 1 (7-ounce) can refrigerated breadstick dough

1. Combine Asiago cheese, sesame seeds, and black pepper in a small bowl. Separate breadstick dough to form 8 sticks, and roll each breadstick in cheese mixture. Bake according to package directions. **Yield:** 8 servings (serving size: 1 breadstick).

CALORIES 99; FAT 3.6g (sat 1.8g, mono 0.9g, poly 0.6g); PROTEIN 4.1g; CARB 12.6g; FIBER 0.4g; CHOL 6mg; IRON 0.7mg; SODIUM 189mg; CALC 77mg

back on track

Reward Yourself

One way to get back on track is to set new goals and give yourself a reward for every small goal you meet. For example, consider rewarding yourself with a movie at the theater (skip the popcorn with butter) every time you lose five pounds or each month you've maintained your weight loss. Simple rewards that recognize your hard work can help keep you motivated and energized.

Chicken, Carrot, and Cucumber Salad

382 calories

We paired this chunky chicken salad with pita wedges, but you can also use pita chips if you'd like. You can purchase them or make your own by spraying pita wedges with cooking spray and baking them at 400° for about 10 minutes.

2 cups chopped cooked chicken breast (about 1 pound)
1¼ cups chopped seeded cucumber
½ cup matchstick-cut carrots
½ cup sliced radishes
⅓ cup chopped green onions
¼ cup light mayonnaise
2 tablespoons chopped fresh cilantro
1 teaspoon bottled minced garlic
¼ teaspoon salt
¼ teaspoon ground cumin
⅛ teaspoon black pepper
4 green leaf lettuce leaves
4 (6-inch) whole-wheat pitas, each cut into 8 wedges

1. Combine first 5 ingredients in a large bowl. Combine mayonnaise and next 5 ingredients in a small bowl, stirring with a whisk. Add mayonnaise mixture to chicken mixture; stir until combined.
2. Place 1 lettuce leaf on each of 4 plates; top each leaf with about 1 cup chicken mixture. Place 8 pita wedges on each serving. **Yield:** 4 servings.

CALORIES 382; FAT 10.4g (sat 2.1g, mono 2.7g, poly 4.3g); PROTEIN 40.7g; CARB 31.4g; FIBER 5.1g; CHOL 102mg; IRON 3mg; SODIUM 621mg; CALC 56mg

a little more...

Pair this salad with a portable piece of fruit. One medium pear contains 95 calories.

quick fix

Not Just For Kids (or Boxers)

Jumping rope requires only one piece of equipment, and you may have a jump rope already lying around—if not, they're an inexpensive investment. That piece of rope can help you blast about 250 calories in 20 minutes.

Superfast Chef Salad

Start with a bag of prechopped romaine lettuce and a rotisserie chicken from the grocery store for an easy, healthy lunch.

10 cups torn or chopped romaine lettuce
 1 cup shredded skinless, boneless rotisserie chicken breast
 ½ cup thinly sliced Texas 1015 or other sweet onion
 ⅓ cup shaved carrot
 1 avocado, seeded, peeled, and sliced
 3 tablespoons crumbled blue cheese
 ½ cup Easy Herb Vinaigrette

1. Arrange 2½ cups lettuce on each of 4 plates. Top lettuce evenly with chicken, onion, carrot, avocado, and blue cheese. Drizzle each serving with 2 tablespoons Easy Herb Vinaigrette; serve immediately. **Yield:** 4 servings.

CALORIES 367; FAT 28.2g (sat 3.4g, mono 15g, poly 6.2g); PROTEIN 18.5g; CARB 12.6g; FIBER 4.6g; CHOL 43mg; IRON 2mg; SODIUM 451mg; CALC 66mg

Easy Herb Vinaigrette

This recipe makes plenty of dressing to keep on hand, so having a salad with dinner is effortless any night of the week.

 9 tablespoons white wine vinegar
 1½ tablespoons wildflower honey
 ½ teaspoon fine sea salt
 1 cup canola oil
 3 tablespoons chopped fresh basil
 3 tablespoons minced fresh chives

1. Combine first 3 ingredients in a medium bowl; slowly whisk in oil until combined. Stir in basil and chives. Store, covered, in refrigerator for up to 5 days. **Yield:** about 1⅔ cups (serving size: 2 tablespoons).

CALORIES 160; FAT 17.2g (sat 1.2g, mono 10.2g, poly 5.1g); PROTEIN 0.1g; CARB 2.1g; FIBER 0.1g; CHOL 0mg; IRON 0mg; SODIUM 89mg; CALC 2mg

a little more...

Serve with a crusty wheat baguette—a 2-ounce serving will add 132 calories.

nutrition note

Is Fat-Free Salad Dressing Best?

Not necessarily. Researchers have long known that fat aids in the absorption of certain vitamins and antioxidants, so some fat (in the form of healthy oils) is a healthy choice for your salad dressings. When you choose a fat-free variety, you may miss out on some of those good-for-you compounds found in the foods you're eating.

Mango and Black Bean Salad

334 calories

The sweet mango brightens the earthiness of the beans and wild rice. Garnish with fresh cilantro.

1½ cups chopped peeled ripe mango
1 cup thinly sliced green onions
½ cup cooked wild or brown rice
3 tablespoons finely chopped fresh cilantro
2 tablespoons roasted tomatillo or fresh salsa
2 tablespoons fresh lime juice
2 tablespoons extra-virgin olive oil
¾ teaspoon salt
¼ teaspoon freshly ground black pepper
1 (15-ounce) can organic no-salt-added black beans, rinsed and drained
Fresh cilantro (optional)

1. Combine all ingredients in a large bowl. Toss gently to mix. Garnish with cilantro, if desired. **Yield:** 3 servings (serving size: about 1⅓ cups).

CALORIES 334; FAT 10.8g (sat 1.4g, mono 6.8g, poly 1.6g); PROTEIN 10.4g; CARB 51g; FIBER 11g; CHOL 0mg; IRON 2.2mg; SODIUM 452mg; CALC 82mg

a little more...

Add ½ cup of steamed or sautéed shrimp to this salad for a larger meal. It'll add 85 calories to your meal.

nutrition note

Canned Beans

Canned beans are a great option for adding protein and fiber to dishes. Organic, no-salt-added beans have the lowest amount of sodium of canned varieties. Plus, rinsing and draining them lowers the beans' sodium by another 40 percent.

Mediterranean Barley Salad

313 calories

This hearty salad packs in more than 8 grams of fiber, which will help keep you feeling full longer.

2¼ cups water
¾ cup uncooked pearl barley
1½ teaspoons grated lemon rind
3 tablespoons fresh lemon juice
2 tablespoons extra-virgin olive oil
½ teaspoon Dijon mustard
1 cup thinly sliced fennel bulb (about 1 small bulb)
⅓ cup chopped fresh parsley
¼ cup finely chopped red onion
¾ teaspoon kosher salt
½ teaspoon coarsely ground black pepper
8 pitted kalamata olives, halved
1 (15-ounce) can cannellini beans, rinsed and drained
⅓ cup chopped walnuts, toasted

1. Bring 2¼ cups water and barley to a boil in a saucepan. Cover, reduce heat, and simmer 25 minutes or until tender and liquid is almost absorbed. Cool to room temperature.

2. Combine lemon rind and next 3 ingredients in a bowl; stir well with a whisk. Add barley, fennel, and next 6 ingredients; toss gently. Cover and refrigerate 30 minutes. Garnish with walnuts just before serving. **Yield:** 4 servings (serving size: 1¼ cups salad and about 4 teaspoons nuts).

CALORIES 313; FAT 16.1g (sat 1.9g, mono 7.5g, poly 6.2g); PROTEIN 6.6g; CARB 38.9g; FIBER 8.2g; CHOL 0mg; IRON 2.9mg; SODIUM 643mg; CALC 79mg

a little more...

Pair this salad with a calcium-rich side, such as a 6-ounce carton of plain fat-free yogurt drizzled with 1 tablespoon honey. This sweet side adds 164 calories and 300 milligrams of calcium—30 percent of the daily recommendation for calcium.

nutrition note

Barley

This ancient grain is perfect for modern cooking. It contains a kind of fiber called beta-glucans, which may help lower levels of total cholesterol, including artery-clogging LDL cholesterol and blood triglycerides.

Moroccan-Spiced Bulgur and Chickpea Salad

394 calories

Fresh mint gives this dish a pleasant aroma. Dried cranberries offer a hint of sweetness. Use any other dried fruit you like in their place: Try golden raisins, currants, dried cherries, or chopped dried apricots. Pair the salad with a kiwifruit (56 calories) for an easily portable side.

3	tablespoons fresh lime juice
1	tablespoon extra-virgin olive oil
½	teaspoon salt
¼	teaspoon ground cumin
¼	teaspoon ground coriander
¼	teaspoon freshly ground black pepper
2	cups boiling water
1⅓	cups uncooked bulgur
½	cup matchstick-cut carrots
⅓	cup dried cranberries
3	tablespoons slivered almonds, toasted
2	teaspoons chopped fresh mint
1	(15½-ounce) can chickpeas (garbanzo beans), drained

1. Combine first 6 ingredients in a large bowl, stirring with a whisk; set aside.
2. Combine 2 cups boiling water and bulgur in a large bowl. Cover and let stand 20 minutes or until liquid is absorbed. Add bulgur, carrots, and next 4 ingredients to juice mixture, and toss well to coat. Cover and chill. **Yield:** 4 servings (serving size: about 1 cup).

CALORIES 338; FAT 8.4g (sat 0.8g, mono 4.9g, poly 2.2g); PROTEIN 10.4g; CARB 59.5g; Fiber 13.7g; CHOL 0mg; IRON 2.8mg; SODIUM 491mg; CALC 65mg

a little more...

Serve yourself a little more of this salad—a 1⅔-cup serving offers 451 calories and 18.2 grams of filling fiber.

nutrition note

Fabulous Fiber

Fiber satisfies. This is because fiber moves through your body more slowly, taking longer to digest than highly refined carbohydrates like white bread and pasta. The result is feeling fuller longer, which can be helpful if you're trying to lose or maintain your weight. The daily recommendation for fiber is 25 grams. One serving of this salad gets you more than half-way to your goal.

Tabbouleh with Chicken and Red Pepper

367 calories

Use rotisserie or leftover chicken for this dish, if you like. If you're making the mixture a few hours or more in advance, store the cucumber and tomato separately and add them close to serving time to keep the salad at its best. Serve with ¼ cup of hummus (93 calories) and a small whole-wheat pita cut into wedges (74 calories) for a flavorful, Middle East–themed light lunch.

½ cup uncooked bulgur
½ cup boiling water
1½ cups diced plum tomato
¾ cup shredded cooked chicken breast
¾ cup minced fresh flat-leaf parsley
½ cup finely chopped red bell pepper
½ cup diced English cucumber
¼ cup minced fresh mint
1½ tablespoons fresh lemon juice
1 tablespoon extra-virgin olive oil
½ teaspoon salt
¼ teaspoon freshly ground black pepper

1. Combine bulgur and ½ cup boiling water in a large bowl. Cover and let stand 15 minutes or until bulgur is tender. Drain well; return bulgur to bowl. Cool.
2. Add tomato and remaining ingredients; toss well. **Yield:** 3 servings (serving size: 1⅔ cups).

CALORIES 200; FAT 6.3g (sat 1.1g, mono 3.9g, poly 0.9g); PROTEIN 14.9g; CARB 22.5g; FIBER 6g; CHOL 29mg; IRON 2.1mg; SODIUM 435mg; CALC 44mg

a little more...

Bulk up this salad by adding an additional ¼ cup of shredded cooked chicken breast. It'll provide an extra 10.9 grams of protein and 58 calories.

Wheat Berry Salad with Goat Cheese

373 calories

Taking a cue from traditional tabbouleh, this dish uses lots of peak-season vegetables, tart lemon juice, and pungent fresh herbs. Serve with multigrain crackers. A serving of 15 crackers provides 120 calories.

1¼ cups wheat berries
2½ cups chopped English cucumber
1½ cups loosely packed chopped arugula
⅔ cup thinly sliced green onions
6 tablespoons minced fresh flat-leaf parsley
1 pint grape tomatoes, halved
1 tablespoon grated lemon rind
3 tablespoons fresh lemon juice
1 teaspoon kosher salt
½ teaspoon freshly ground black pepper
½ teaspoon sugar
2 tablespoons extra-virgin olive oil
¾ cup (3 ounces) crumbled goat cheese

1. Place wheat berries in a medium bowl; cover with water to 2 inches above wheat berries. Cover and let stand 8 hours. Drain.
2. Place wheat berries in a medium saucepan; cover with water to 2 inches above wheat berries. Bring to a boil, reduce heat, and cook, uncovered, 1 hour or until tender. Drain and rinse with cold water; drain well. Place wheat berries in a large bowl; add cucumber and next 4 ingredients.
3. Combine rind and next 4 ingredients in a bowl; gradually add oil, stirring constantly with a whisk. Drizzle dressing over salad; toss well to coat. Stir in cheese. Let stand at least 30 minutes; serve at room temperature. **Yield:** 6 servings (serving size: about 1⅓ cups).

CALORIES 253; FAT 9.7g (sat 3.7g, mono 4.4g, poly 0.9g); PROTEIN 9.2g; CARB 35.7g; FIBER 6.8g; CHOL 11mg; IRON 1.2mg; SODIUM 401mg; CALC 79mg

a little more...

Serve yourself a heartier portion of this salad. A 1½-cup serving provides 304 calories. You could also add another tablespoon of crumbled goat cheese to your serving for a richer flavor. That addition will add 19 calories.

quick fix

Lunch-Hour Gym Class

If you can, head to the gym (or home) one day a week and get in an hour of aerobics. This lunchtime sweat session can burn over 400 calories.

Tortellini Pepperoncini Salad

378 calories

With spicy peppers, sweet cherry tomatoes, earthy beans, and lots of fresh herbs, this well-balanced recipe is a meal in itself. Pair it with a fresh medium orange (62 calories) for a sweet finish to this salad.

1 (9-ounce) package fresh cheese tortellini
2 cups halved cherry tomatoes
2 cups fresh spinach leaves, coarsely chopped
½ cup chopped pepperoncini peppers
6 tablespoons (1½ ounces) preshredded fresh Parmesan cheese
¼ cup capers
¼ cup chopped fresh basil
1 (16-ounce) can navy beans
2 tablespoons fresh lemon juice
1½ tablespoons extra-virgin olive oil

1. Cook pasta according to package directions, omitting salt and fat.
2. While pasta cooks, combine tomatoes and next 6 ingredients in a large bowl. Drain pasta; rinse with cold water. Add pasta, juice, and oil to tomato mixture; toss gently. Serve immediately. **Yield:** 5 servings (serving size: about 1½ cups).

CALORIES 316; FAT 10.3g (sat 3.2g, mono 3.3g, poly 0.6g); PROTEIN 15.1g; CARB 41.9g; FIBER 5.3g; CHOL 22mg; IRON 1.7mg; SODIUM 929mg; CALC 171mg

a little more...

Stir in ½ cup of chopped cooked chicken breast for an additional 116 calories and 22 grams of protein per serving.

nutrition note

Fresh Herbs

Fresh herbs can take a dish from good to great. They infuse a dish with unparalleled aromas and flavors, while contributing antioxidants in a virtually zero-calorie package.

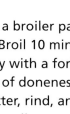

Cornmeal-Crusted Tilapia Sandwiches with Lime Butter

345 calories

Broiling the fish creates a delicious crunchy, browned exterior.

3 tablespoons yellow cornmeal
1 tablespoon chili powder
1 teaspoon ground cumin
½ teaspoon salt
½ teaspoon ground coriander
⅛ teaspoon ground red pepper
4 (6-ounce) tilapia fillets
Cooking spray
2 tablespoons butter, softened
1 teaspoon grated lime rind
½ teaspoon fresh lime juice
4 (1½-ounce) French bread rolls, toasted
4 (¼-inch-thick) slices tomato
1 cup shredded red leaf lettuce

1. Preheat broiler.
2. Combine first 6 ingredients in a shallow dish. Coat both sides of fish with cooking spray. Dredge fish in cornmeal mixture.

3. Place fish on a broiler pan coated with cooking spray. Broil 10 minutes or until fish flakes easily with a fork or until desired degree of doneness.
4. Combine butter, rind, and juice in a small bowl; stir well.
5. Spread 1½ teaspoons butter mixture over cut side of each of 4 roll tops. Place 1 fillet, 1 tomato slice, and ¼ cup lettuce on each of 4 roll bottoms. Place top halves of rolls on sandwiches. Yield: 4 servings (serving size: 1 sandwich).

CALORIES 345; FAT 9.9g (sat 4.6g, mono 2.3g, poly 1g); PROTEIN 39.2g; CARB 26.3g; FIBER 2g; CHOL 100mg; IRON 2.6mg; SODIUM 708mg; CALC 68mg

a little more...

Plate this sandwich with ½ cup of grapes (60 calories) and ½ cup of coleslaw (100 calories) for a full lunch.

nutrition note

Mimicking Frying

Using the broiler to mimic frying is one way to get the same crisp, crunchy exterior and moist interior that deep-frying provides. However, this method involves considerable less oil (in this recipe, zero oil since cooking spray is used) and is certainly healthier. The key is coating the food in batter or a breadcrumb/cornmeal mixture. That coating insulates the food but also browns and crisps under the high heat of the broiler, giving it a wonderful crunch.

Tuna Pan Bagnat

398 calories

A favorite in southern France, pan bagnat (pan ban-YAH) means "bathed bread." The bread in this sandwich is meant to absorb some liquid from the filling, so it's fine to completely assemble it ahead of time. Serve with 1 ounce (about 13 chips) of baked barbecue chips (150 calories) to complete the meal.

- ⅓ cup finely chopped red onion
- 2 tablespoons chopped pitted niçoise olives
- 1 tablespoon fresh lemon juice
- ¼ teaspoon kosher salt
- ¼ teaspoon freshly ground black pepper
- 1 (6-ounce) can premium tuna, packed in oil, drained
- 1 hard-cooked large egg, chopped
- ¼ cup thinly sliced fresh basil
- 2 teaspoons extra-virgin olive oil
- 1 (8-ounce) whole-wheat French bread baguette
- 1 garlic clove, halved
- 1 cup thinly sliced plum tomato (about 1)

1. Combine first 7 ingredients in a medium bowl. Combine basil and oil; stir with a whisk. Cut bread in half horizontally. Hollow out top and bottom halves of bread, leaving a 1-inch-thick shell; reserve torn bread for another use. Rub cut sides of garlic clove over cut sides of bread; discard garlic. Drizzle basil mixture evenly over cut sides of bread. Spoon tuna mixture on bottom half of baguette. Arrange tomato slices over tuna mixture. Cover with top half of baguette. Wrap filled baguette in plastic wrap, and let stand for 20 minutes. Cut filled baguette into 4 (3-inch) equal portions. **Yield:** 4 servings (serving size: 1 sandwich).

CALORIES 248; FAT 9.3g (sat 1.4g, mono 4.6g, poly 2g); PROTEIN 14.5g; CARB 26.3g; FIBER 2.2g; CHOL 63mg; IRON 2mg; SODIUM 589mg; CALC 84mg

a little more...

Substitute baked sweet potato fries for the chips. A serving of 20 fries will provide 250 calories.

nutrition note

Canned Tuna

Canned tuna is an economical source of vitamin D. Three ounces contain approximately 50 percent of your daily vitamin D requirement. Concern has been raised about mercury levels in some fish and shellfish, such as tuna. However most experts agree that the benefits of moderate fish consumption (up to 12 ounces of low-mercury fish per week) far outweigh the risks.

Lobster Wraps with Lemon Mayonnaise

Flatbread replaces buttered rolls in this take on the New England classic.

371 calories

LEMON MAYONNAISE
- ¼ cup light mayonnaise
- 2 tablespoons chopped fresh chives
- 1 teaspoon fresh lemon juice
- ⅛ teaspoon freshly ground black pepper

REMAINING INGREDIENTS
- ¾ cup chopped seeded tomato (about 1 medium)
- 4 (4-ounce) lobster tails, cooked and chopped
- 4 (2.8-ounce) whole-wheat flatbreads (such as Flatout)
- 8 Bibb lettuce leaves

1. To prepare lemon mayonnaise, combine first 4 ingredients; stir well.

2. Combine lemon mayonnaise, tomato, and lobster; stir well. Divide lobster mixture evenly among flatbreads. Top each serving with 2 lettuce leaves. Roll up jelly-roll fashion. **Yield:** 4 servings (serving size: 1 wrap).

CALORIES 371; FAT 8.6g (sat 1g, mono 1.5g, poly 0.6g); PROTEIN 31g; CARB 41.7g; FIBER 3.6g; CHOL 113mg; IRON 0.7mg; SODIUM 1098mg; CALC 66mg

a little more...

Pair this wrap with roasted baked potato wedges for a tasty side. You can use a convenient frozen option (such as Simply Potatoes) to save prep time. A 1-cup serving will add 100 calories to this meal.

back on track

Use Your Measuring Cups

A big component of weight loss and weight maintenance is portion control. If you've had a setback, the problem could be that you're dishing up larger portions without realizing it. One way to check is to pull out your measuring cups and spoons and use them when cooking and portioning. It'll get you acquainted with what a serving should look like on your plate. Once your eyes get used to the amounts again, you can begin eyeballing your serving sizes again.

Pan-Seared Shrimp Po' Boys

397 calories

This New Orleans classic, featuring a homemade five-ingredient tartar sauce made with pantry staples, takes only 20 minutes to prepare. Using salt-free Cajun seasoning reduces the sodium in this dish without sacrificing any of the flavor.

- ⅓ cup reduced-fat mayonnaise
- 2 tablespoons sweet pickle relish
- 1 tablespoon chopped shallots
- 1 teaspoon capers, chopped
- ¼ teaspoon hot pepper sauce (such as Tabasco)
- 1 pound peeled and deveined large shrimp
- 1½ teaspoons salt-free Cajun seasoning
- 2 teaspoons olive oil
- 4 (2½-ounce) hoagie rolls
- ½ cup shredded romaine lettuce
- 8 thin slices tomato
- 4 thin slices red onion (optional)

1. Combine first 5 ingredients in a small bowl. Heat a large nonstick skillet over medium-high heat. Combine shrimp and Cajun seasoning in a bowl; toss well. Add olive oil to pan, and swirl to coat. Add shrimp to pan; cook 2 minutes on each side or until done.

2. Cut each roll in half horizontally. Top bottom half of each roll with 2 table-spoons lettuce, 2 tomato slices, 1 onion slice, if desired, and one-fourth of shrimp. Spread top half of each roll with about 2 tablespoons mayonnaise mixture; place on top of sandwich. **Yield:** 4 servings (serving size: 1 sandwich).

CALORIES 397; FAT 12.1g (sat 2.8g, mono 4.6g, poly 3.2g); PROTEIN 30.6g; CARB 43.4g; FIBER 2.5g; CHOL 172mg; IRON 4.4mg; SODIUM 944mg; CALC 150mg

a little more...

Pair this with crunchy Carrot and Cabbage Slaw. One serving will add 45 calories to this meal.

Carrot and Cabbage Slaw

- 3 tablespoons reduced-fat mayonnaise
- 1 tablespoon cider vinegar
- ¼ teaspoon celery seeds
- 4 cups shredded green cabbage
- 1 cup shredded carrot

1. Combine mayonnaise, cider vinegar, and celery seeds in a large bowl, stirring with a whisk. Add cabbage and carrot to mayonnaise mixture; stir well to combine. **Yield:** 4 servings.

CALORIES 45; FAT 1.7g (sat 0g, mono 0g, poly 0.8g); PROTEIN 1.2g; CARB 8.3g; FIBER 2.5g; CHOL 0mg; IRON 0.5mg; SODIUM 129mg; CALC 40mg

back on track

Weight Training

If lifting weights isn't currently part of your exercise plan, you may want to consider adding it. The reason: The more muscle you have, the more calories you'll burn. Muscle is an active tissue that requires energy to work properly, even at rest. Fat does not. Research has shown that those who alter their diet and lift weights lose more weight than those who only alter their diet.

Mr. Stripey Tomato, Arugula, and Pancetta Sandwiches

343 calories

Pancetta is Italian cured bacon; substitute domestic cured bacon, if necessary. You can prepare the mayonnaise mixture and cook the pancetta up to one day ahead. Pair this sandwich with 1 cup of fresh diced honeydew (61 calories).

2   tablespoons light mayonnaise
1   tablespoon minced shallots
2   teaspoons Dijon mustard
½   teaspoon minced fresh sage
2   ounces pancetta, cut into 8 thin
     slices
Cooking spray
8   (1-ounce) slices rustic sourdough
     bread, toasted
4   medium Mr. Stripey tomatoes or
     another heirloom tomato, each cut
     into 4 (½-inch-thick) slices
1   cup arugula

1. Preheat oven to 400°.
2. Combine first 4 ingredients in a bowl, stirring well.

3. Arrange pancetta in a single layer on a baking sheet coated with cooking spray. Bake at 400° for 8 minutes or until crisp. Drain on paper towels.
4. Spread mayonnaise mixture evenly over bread slices. Top each of 4 bread slices with 2 pancetta slices, 4 tomato slices, and ¼ cup arugula. Top sandwiches with remaining 4 bread slices. **Yield:** 4 servings (serving size: 1 sandwich).

CALORIES 282; FAT 8.7g (sat 2.8g, mono 1.7g, poly 4.1g); PROTEIN 10.5g; CARB 41.9g; FIBER 3.5g; CHOL 13mg; IRON 3mg; SODIUM 699mg; CALC 44mg

a little more...
Serve with veggie chips, which will add 150 calories per 1-ounce serving (about 14 chips).

nutrition note

Light Mayo

Compared to full-fat mayo, light offers real nutritional savings— 50 fewer calories and a savings of 0.5 grams of saturated fat per tablespoon.

Prosciutto, Lettuce, and Tomato Sandwiches

344 calories

The grocery deli will slice prosciutto in very thin pieces, making three ounces more than enough for four sandwiches. For a zesty and pretty garnish, attach 1 small sweet gherkin pickle (11 calories each) to the top of each sandwich with a toothpick. A toss-together fruit salad makes a speedy side. Combine 1 teaspoon fresh lime rind, 1 tablespoon fresh lime juice, 1 tablespoon honey, and a dash of salt; drizzle over 4 cups mixed precut fruit (such as watermelon, cantaloupe, and grapes). One cup provides 90 calories.

8 (1-ounce) slices 100% whole-grain bread
¼ cup canola mayonnaise
2 tablespoons chopped fresh basil
1 teaspoon Dijon mustard
1 small garlic clove, minced
1 cup baby romaine lettuce leaves
8 (¼-inch-thick) slices tomato
3 ounces very thin slices prosciutto

1. Preheat broiler.
2. Arrange bread slices in a single layer on a baking sheet. Broil bread 2 minutes on each side or until toasted.

3. Combine mayonnaise and next 3 ingredients; spread mayonnaise mixture evenly over 4 bread slices. Layer ¼ cup lettuce and 2 tomato slices over each serving; top evenly with prosciutto and remaining bread slices. **Yield:** 4 servings (serving size: 1 sandwich).

CALORIES 243; FAT 9.4g (sat 1.4g, mono 4.6g, poly 2.4g); PROTEIN 11.8g; CARB 28.4g; FIBER 4.3g; CHOL 19mg; IRON 2.5mg; SODIUM 808mg; CALC 62mg

a little more...

Pair with ½ cup of shelled edamame for an additional 100 calories.

nutrition note

Whole-Grain Bread

The U.S. Department of Agriculture recommends that half the grains you eat each day should be whole grains. One way to meet your needs is by choosing whole-grain breads. You'll get antioxidants, vitamins, and minerals as well as a healthy dose of fiber. One way to identify whole grains is to look for "100% whole grain" or "100% whole wheat" on the package. If you don't see that, check the ingredient list. The first ingredient should be whole-wheat flour, whole grain, whole oats, or whole rye.

Cuban Sandwiches

A citrus-laced marinade and a tangy relish add big flavor to this Latin classic.

397 calories

- 3 tablespoons extra-virgin olive oil
- ½ cup minced onion
- ½ teaspoon kosher salt
- ½ teaspoon dried oregano
- ½ teaspoon freshly ground black pepper
- 6 garlic cloves, minced
- ¾ cup fresh orange juice
- 2 tablespoons fresh lime juice
- 8 ounces pork tenderloin
- Cooking spray
- ½ cup finely chopped dill pickle
- 2 tablespoons prepared mustard
- 2 teaspoons extra-virgin olive oil
- 4 (3-inch) pieces Cuban bread, cut in half horizontally
- 8 thin slices deli less-sodium ham (about 3 ounces)
- 4 (1-ounce) slices reduced-fat Swiss cheese
- 1 cup baby spinach

1. Heat 3 tablespoons olive oil in a small skillet over medium-high heat. Add onion and next 4 ingredients; sauté 3 minutes or until onion is tender. Remove from heat; stir in orange juice and lime juice. Reserve 2 tablespoons juice mixture; cover and refrigerate. Combine remaining juice mixture and pork in a large zip-top plastic bag; seal. Marinate pork mixture in refrigerator at least 4 hours or overnight.
2. Prepare grill to medium-high heat.
3. Remove pork from bag; discard marinade. Place pork on grill rack coated with cooking spray; grill 15 minutes or until thermometer registers 155° (slightly pink), turning occasionally. Remove pork from grill. Cover loosely with foil; let stand 10 minutes. Cut pork into 16 thin slices.
4. Combine pickle, reserved 2 tablespoons juice mixture, mustard, and 2 teaspoons oil in a small bowl; stir until well blended.
5. Hollow out top and bottom halves of bread, leaving a ½-inch-thick shell; reserve torn bread for another use. Spread 2 teaspoons pickle mixture over cut side of each half. Arrange 4 pork slices, 2 ham slices, 1 cheese slice, and ¼ cup spinach on each bottom half of bread; cover with top halves.
6. Heat a large nonstick grill pan over medium-high heat. Coat pan with cooking spray. Add sandwiches to pan. Place a cast-iron or heavy skillet on top of sandwiches; press gently to flatten. Cook 4 minutes on each side or until cheese melts and bread is toasted (leave cast-iron skillet on sandwiches while they cook). **Yield:** 4 servings (serving size: 1 sandwich).

CALORIES 397; FAT 13.5g (sat 4.4g, mono 4.6g, poly 1.7g); PROTEIN 30.3g; CARB 34.8g; FIBER 1.8g; CHOL 43mg; IRON 2.9mg; SODIUM 984mg; CALC 398mg

a little more...

Pair this savory sandwich with a cup of fresh mango, which adds 107 calories, for a truly Cuban lunch.

nutrition note

Kosher Salt

Using kosher salt can be a great way to cut back on sodium. Because of its larger crystal size, a teaspoon of kosher salt contains almost 25 percent less sodium than ordinary table salt. Plus, it's inexpensive and easy to find in most grocery stores.

Muffulettas

These sandwiches can be prepared the day before and brown-bagged for lunch. The olive salad—which some consider the best part—will moisten the bread overnight.

352 calories

1½ cups bottled giardiniera, drained and chopped (about 6 ounces)
2 tablespoons red wine vinegar
2 tablespoons extra-virgin olive oil
10 pimiento-stuffed manzanilla (or green) olives, chopped
1 garlic clove, minced
4 (2-ounce) Kaiser rolls, cut in half horizontally
4 (½-ounce) slices reduced-fat provolone cheese
4 ounces skinless, boneless rotisserie chicken breast, sliced (about 1 breast)
4 thin slices Genoa salami (about 1½ ounces)
4 thin slices ham (about 2 ounces)

1. Combine first 5 ingredients in a bowl; mix well.
2. Layer bottom half of each roll with 1 provolone cheese slice, 1 ounce chicken, 1 salami slice, and 1 ham slice; top each portion with about ⅓ cup olive mixture and top halves of rolls. Wrap each sandwich tightly in plastic wrap; chill at least 1 hour or overnight. Remove plastic wrap; cut each sandwich in half. **Yield:** 4 servings (serving size: 2 sandwich halves).

CALORIES 352; FAT 16.9g (sat 4.5g, mono 9.1g, poly 2g); PROTEIN 22.2g; CARB 27.1g; FIBER 1.2g; CHOL 47mg; IRON 2.7mg; SODIUM 947mg; CALC 166mg

a little more...

Serve with 1 cup of green grapes for an additional 110 calories.

nutrition note

A Lighter Choice

A traditional muffuletta can contain more than 1,200 calories and more than 4,000 milligrams of sodium. By using reduced-fat cheese, a smaller amount of all the salty meats, and keeping the amount of olive salad added to the sandwich to a reasonable ⅓ cup (which still provides loads of flavor), we were able to make this previously special-occasion sandwich more of an everyday option.

Rosemary Chicken Salad Sandwiches

360 calories

This chicken salad doesn't take long to assemble, and it's an ideal make-ahead meal since it stores well in the refrigerator.

- **3** cups chopped roasted skinless, boneless chicken breast (about ¾ pound)
- **⅓** cup chopped green onions
- **¼** cup chopped smoked almonds
- **¼** cup plain fat-free yogurt
- **¼** cup light mayonnaise
- **1** teaspoon chopped fresh rosemary
- **1** teaspoon Dijon mustard
- **⅛** teaspoon salt
- **⅛** teaspoon freshly ground black pepper
- **10** slices whole-grain bread

1. Combine first 9 ingredients, stirring well. Spread about ⅔ cup chicken mixture over each of 5 bread slices, and top with remaining bread slices. Cut sandwiches in half. **Yield:** 5 servings (serving size: 1 sandwich).

CALORIES 360; FAT 11.6g (sat 2.1g, mono 3.5g, poly 1.8g); PROTEIN 33.6g; CARB: 29.9g; FIBER 4.4g; CHOL 76mg; IRON 2.9mg; SODIUM 529mg; CALC 104mg

a little more...

Serve with 1 cup of fresh cubed watermelon—it'll add 46 calories.

nutrition note

Almonds

Just 1 ounce of almonds, which is about the size of a small handful (about 24 nuts), provides about 20 percent of your daily magnesium needs. Magnesium plays a vital role in hundreds of processes, including muscle and nerve function; regulation of metabolism, heart rate, and blood pressure; and bone health.

Chicken Saté Wraps

393 calories

Coconut milk, curry powder, and peanut butter bring Indonesian flair to a quick-fix sandwich. Pack an apple with your lunch (72 calories) to have on the side.

Cooking spray
½ cup matchstick-cut carrots
⅓ cup chopped green onions
⅔ cup light coconut milk
3 tablespoons creamy peanut butter
1 tablespoon lower-sodium soy sauce
1 tablespoon rice vinegar
1 teaspoon curry powder
⅛ teaspoon ground red pepper
2 cups shredded skinless, boneless rotisserie chicken breast
4 (8-inch) fat-free flour tortillas
1⅓ cups packaged angel hair slaw

1. Heat a large nonstick skillet over medium-high heat. Coat pan with cooking spray. Add carrots and onions; sauté 1 minute. Stir in coconut milk and next 5 ingredients; cook 30 seconds, stirring constantly. Add chicken; cook 1 minute, stirring to coat. Remove from heat; cool. Warm tortillas according to package directions. Spoon about ½ cup chicken mixture down center of each tortilla, and top each with ⅓ cup angel hair slaw. Roll up. Cover and chill. **Yield:** 4 servings (serving size: 1 wrap).

CALORIES 321; FAT 10.1g (sat 3.3g, mono 3.7g, poly 2.1g); PROTEIN 24.1g; CARB: 25.5g; FIBER 4.3g; CHOL 49mg; IRON 0.9mg; SODIUM 844mg; CALC 37mg

a little more...

Serve baked chips on the side. A 1-ounce serving will add 150 calories to the meal.

nutrition note

Soy Sauce

Soy sauce is skinny on calories, but hefty on sodium. By selecting the "lite" version, you'll save 315 milligrams of sodium per tablespoon while still adding tons of flavor to your meal.

135

Caprese Wraps with Chicken

Pick up a rotisserie chicken and assemble this hearty sandwich for a quick and easy lunch any day of the week.

2 tablespoons olive oil
2 tablespoons white wine vinegar
¼ teaspoon kosher salt
¼ teaspoon black pepper
4 cups prechopped hearts of romaine lettuce
1½ cups shredded skinless, boneless rotisserie chicken breast
¾ cup (3 ounces) fresh mozzarella cheese, chopped
½ cup fresh basil leaves, torn
1 pint cherry tomatoes, quartered
Cooking spray
4 (2.8-ounce) multigrain flatbreads (such as Flatout)
1 large garlic clove, halved

1. Combine first 4 ingredients in a large bowl, stirring with a whisk. Add lettuce and next 4 ingredients, tossing to coat.
2. Heat a large nonstick skillet over medium-high heat. Coat pan with cooking spray. Working with 1 flatbread at a time, cook bread 1 minute on each side or until toasted. Rub 1 side of each flatbread with cut sides of garlic; discard garlic. Arrange 1½ cups chicken mixture in center of each flatbread; roll up.
Yield: 4 servings (serving size: 1 wrap).

CALORIES 328; FAT 15.9g (sat 4.5g, mono 6.2g, poly 2.7g); PROTEIN 30.3g; CARB 22g; FIBER 9.5g; CHOL 61mg; IRON 2.9mg; SODIUM 573mg; CALC 180mg

a little more...

Pack an easily portable banana to have with your lunch. A medium banana will add 110 calories to your meal.

nutrition note

Nonstick Skillets

For light cooking, a nonstick skillet is essential because it requires little added fat. It's ideal for sautéing delicate foods like fish, cooking vegetables, making grilled cheese sandwiches (or any sandwich), and is necessary for scrambling eggs and preparing pancakes. But the nonstick surface is relatively delicate and shouldn't be placed over high heat. And although proper care can extend its shelf life, the nonstick coating will eventually wear down over time and you'll need to replace your pan.

Grilled Chicken and Tapenade Sandwiches

369 calories

1½ cups diced seeded tomato
2 tablespoons finely chopped pitted kalamata olives
1 tablespoon chopped fresh basil
1 tablespoon chopped fresh flat-leaf parsley
2 tablespoons balsamic vinegar
1 teaspoon chopped fresh oregano
½ teaspoon minced garlic
5 teaspoons extra-virgin olive oil, divided
1 pound skinless, boneless chicken breast
½ teaspoon kosher salt, divided
½ teaspoon freshly ground black pepper
   Cooking spray
¼ cup (1 ounce) crumbled feta cheese
4 (2-ounce) ciabatta sandwich rolls, halved

1. Combine first 7 ingredients in a small bowl. Add 2 teaspoons oil; toss gently to combine. Let stand 15 minutes.
2. Prepare grill.
3. Brush chicken evenly with remaining 1 tablespoon oil, and sprinkle with ¼ teaspoon salt and pepper. Place chicken on grill rack coated with cooking spray; grill 6 minutes on each side or until chicken is done. Remove from grill. Let stand 5 minutes before slicing thinly.
4. Add cheese and remaining ¼ teaspoon salt to tomato mixture; stir gently to combine. Arrange sliced chicken evenly on bottom halves of rolls. Top each serving with one-fourth of tomato mixture, and cover with top halves of rolls. Serve immediately. **Yield:** 4 servings (serving size: 1 sandwich).

CALORIES 369; FAT 12.3g (sat 3g, mono 7g, poly 1.6g); PROTEIN 33.2g; CARB 30.1g; FIBER 1.5g; CHOL 79mg; IRON 2.7mg; SODIUM 815mg; CALC 63mg

a little more...

You can prepare the Grilled Vegetable Skewers right alongside the chicken for an easy 58-calorie side.

Grilled Vegetable Skewers

2 zucchini, cut into 1½-inch pieces
1 red bell pepper, cut into 1½-inch pieces
1 red onion, cut into 1½-inch pieces
2 teaspoons olive oil
½ teaspoon kosher salt
¼ teaspoon freshly ground black pepper
1 tablespoon balsamic vinegar

1. Thread vegetables alternately onto each of 4 skewers; brush with oil, and sprinkle with salt and pepper. Grill 15 minutes or until crisp-tender and lightly charred. Brush evenly with balsamic vinegar just before serving. **Yield:** 4 servings (serving size: 1 skewer).

CALORIES 58; FAT 2.6g (sat 0.4g, mono 1.7g, poly 0.4g); PROTEIN 1.8g; CARB 8.4g; FIBER 2.2g; CHOL 0mg; IRON 0.6mg; SODIUM 248mg; CALC 25mg

nutrition note

Grilling

Grilling creates charred edges, telltale grill marks, and smoky, robust taste with minimal effort—the heat of the fire does all the work. And all these delicious qualities come with little or no added fat, making this one of the easiest and most healthful cooking methods.

Grilled Turkey and Ham Sandwiches

397 calories

Enjoy with ½ cup of carrot sticks (25 calories) and ¾ cup of less-sodium tomato soup (135 calories) for a complete meal.

1 tablespoon light mayonnaise
1 teaspoon Dijon mustard
8 (1-ounce) slices country white bread
4 (1-ounce) slices deli less-sodium turkey breast
4 (½-ounce) slices deli less-sodium ham
4 (½-ounce) slices reduced-fat cheddar cheese
8 (¼-inch-thick) slices tomato
Cooking spray

1. Combine mayonnaise and mustard in a small bowl. Spread about 1 teaspoon mayonnaise mixture over 1 side of each of 4 bread slices. Top each slice with 1 turkey slice, 1 ham slice, 1 cheese slice, and 2 tomato slices. Top with remaining bread slices.
2. Heat a large nonstick skillet over medium heat. Coat pan with cooking spray. Add sandwiches to pan; cook 4 minutes or until lightly browned. Turn sandwiches over; cook 2 minutes or until cheese melts. **Yield:** 4 servings (serving size: 1 sandwich).

CALORIES 237; FAT 5.8g (sat 1.8g, mono 0.9g, poly 0.9g); PROTEIN 18.4g; CARB 29.1g; FIBER 0.4g; CHOL 28mg; IRON 1.1mg; SODIUM 781mg; CALC 166mg

a little more...

Add an extra slice of cheese for a cheesier, meltier sandwich. Another ½-ounce slice will add 46 calories.

nutrition note

Lower-Salt Meats

It can be hard to find packaged deli meats that aren't loaded with sodium. Some of these meats are cured in salt, which naturally increases the sodium content. But seeking out lower-sodium meats can lead to a real nutritional savings—some contain half the sodium of regular deli meats. If a lower-sodium variety isn't available in your grocery store (in the prepackaged section or at the deli counter), read the nutrition label to find a brand with the lowest amount of sodium per serving—ideally less than 350 milligrams per 2-ounce serving.

Turkey Panini with Watercress and Citrus Aioli

354 calories

Take your average turkey sandwich to the next level with a citrusy spread and a few minutes on the panini press. Pair with a tangerine (50 calories) for another hit of citrus flavor.

2 **tablespoons canola mayonnaise**
¼ **teaspoon grated lime rind**
¼ **teaspoon grated lemon rind**
1 **teaspoon fresh lemon juice**
¼ **teaspoon freshly ground black pepper**
1 **garlic clove, minced**
8 **(1-ounce) slices white bread**
½ **pound deli-sliced smoked turkey (such as Boar's Head)**
2 **cups trimmed watercress**
4 **(½-ounce) slices provolone cheese**
  Cooking spray

1. Heat a grill pan over medium-high heat.
2. Combine first 6 ingredients; spread evenly over 4 bread slices. Top evenly with turkey, watercress, cheese, and remaining 4 bread slices.

3. Coat grill pan with cooking spray. Arrange 2 sandwiches in pan. Place a cast-iron or heavy skillet on top of sandwiches; press gently to flatten. Cook 2 minutes on each side (leave cast-iron skillet on sandwiches while they cook). Repeat procedure with remaining 2 sandwiches. **Yield:** 4 servings (serving size: 1 sandwich).

CALORIES 304; FAT 11.8g (sat 2.7g, mono 2.8g, poly 3.6g); PROTEIN 21.3g; CARB 29g; FIBER 1.2g; CHOL 38mg; IRON 2mg; SODIUM 810mg; CALC 210mg

a little more...

Add a 6-ounce carton of fat-free yogurt in your favorite flavor for an additional 100 calories.

nutrition note

Canola Mayonnaise

Mayonnaise made with canola oil is a healthy choice. One tablespoon contains 45 calories (55 less than a tablespoon of full-fat mayonnaise) and no saturated fat. Plus, since it's made with canola oil, it's naturally rich in omega-3s.

143

Grown-Up Grilled Cheese Sandwiches

This luscious veggie-packed sandwich feels like an indulgence. Serve with a zesty dill pickle spear (6 calories).

Cooking spray
1 cup vertically sliced red onion
1 large garlic clove, minced
1 cup (4 ounces) reduced-fat shredded sharp white cheddar cheese (such as Cracker Barrel)
8 (1½-ounce) slices hearty white bread (such as Pepperidge Farm)
2 cups fresh spinach leaves
8 (¼-inch-thick) slices tomato
6 slices center-cut bacon, cooked

1. Heat a large nonstick skillet over medium-low heat. Coat pan with cooking spray. Add 1 cup onion and garlic; cook 10 minutes or until tender and golden brown, stirring occasionally.
2. Sprinkle 2 tablespoons cheese over each of 4 bread slices. Top each slice with ½ cup spinach, 2 tomato slices, 2 tablespoons onion mixture, and 1½ bacon slices. Sprinkle each with 2 tablespoons cheese; top with remaining 4 bread slices.
3. Heat pan over medium heat. Coat pan with cooking spray. Place sandwiches in pan, and cook 3 minutes on each side or until golden brown and cheese melts.
Yield: 4 servings (serving size: 1 sandwich).

CALORIES 376; FAT 11g (sat 5.3g, mono 4.8g, poly 0.6g); PROTEIN 20.2g; CARB 50.3g; FIBER 3.3g; CHOL 24mg; IRON 2.9mg; SODIUM 876mg; CALC 308mg

a little more...

For a weekend meal, pair the sandwich with a sweet-tart hard cider. A 12-ounce bottle will add 172 calories to this lunch.

quick fix

Basketball

Call some friends or grab your kids and head outside for a game of basketball. Thirty minutes of shooting hoops can burn more than 200 calories.

Grilled Vegetable Pitas with Goat Cheese and Pesto Mayo

Pair this with baked potato chips. A 1-ounce serving will add 150 calories to the meal.

4   (4-inch) portobello mushroom caps (about ½ pound)
2   medium red bell peppers, quartered
1   medium Vidalia or other sweet onion, cut into 4 slices
    Cooking spray
¼   teaspoon kosher salt
⅛   teaspoon freshly ground black pepper
2¼ teaspoons balsamic vinegar
¼   cup reduced-fat mayonnaise
1   tablespoon commercial pesto
2   whole-wheat pitas, cut in half
4   green leaf lettuce leaves
½   cup (2 ounces) crumbled goat cheese

1. Prepare grill to medium-high heat.
2. Arrange mushrooms, gill sides up; bell pepper quarters; and onion slices on a baking sheet. Coat vegetables with cooking spray. Sprinkle evenly with salt and black pepper. Drizzle vinegar over mushrooms. Place vegetables on grill rack; grill 5 minutes on each side or until tender.
3. Combine mayonnaise and pesto. Spread 1 tablespoon mayonnaise mixture into each pita half. Stuff each pita half with 1 lettuce leaf, one-fourth of grilled vegetables, and 2 tablespoons cheese. Serve immediately. **Yield:** 4 servings (serving size: 1 stuffed pita half).

CALORIES 220; FAT 7.3g (sat 2.5g, mono 1.6g, poly 1.6g); PROTEIN 8.9g; CARB 33.7g; FIBER 5.8g; CHOL 7mg; IRON 2.1mg; SODIUM 505mg; CALC 62mg

a little more…

This sandwich would also be great paired with the Carrot and Cabbage Slaw on page 122. That addition will provide 45 calories.

quick fix

Child's Play

Remember how as a child you didn't "exercise"? Exercise was effortless and as natural as breathing. Experts recommend bringing back that sense of fun and freedom to help you incorporate fitness into your daily life. Try it. During a 30-minute game of kickball or 30 minutes of rollerskating or rollerblading, you'll burn about 250 calories.

Butternut Squash Soup

338 calories

Serve this with a simple side salad made of 1 cup of spinach, 1 thin slice of onion, and 1 tablespoon of your favorite light vinaigrette (41 calories) to round out this lunch.

SOUP

1	**tablespoon butter**
3½	**cups cubed peeled butternut squash (about 1½ pounds)**
¾	**cup chopped carrot**
½	**cup chopped sweet onion**
2½	**cups fat-free, lower-sodium chicken broth**
¼	**cup half-and-half**
⅛	**teaspoon salt**

TOASTS

4	**(1-ounce) slices French bread**
3	**ounces thinly sliced Swiss cheese**

1. To prepare soup, melt butter in a large saucepan over medium-high heat. Add squash, carrot, and onion; sauté 12 minutes. Add chicken broth, and bring to a boil. Cover, reduce heat, and simmer 30 minutes. Remove from heat; stir in half-and-half and salt.

2. Preheat broiler.

3. Place squash mixture in a blender. Remove center piece of blender lid (to allow steam to escape), and secure blender lid on blender. Place a clean towel over opening in blender lid (to avoid splatters). Blend until smooth.

4. To prepare toasts, arrange French bread on a baking sheet. Broil 1 minute or until lightly toasted. Turn bread over, and top evenly with Swiss cheese. Broil 1 minute or until bubbly. Serve toasts with soup. **Yield:** 4 servings (serving size: about 1 cup soup and 1 toast).

CALORIES 297; FAT 10.7g (sat 6.7g, mono 2.3g, poly 0.4g); PROTEIN 11.8g; CARB 42.4g; FIBER 4.9g; CHOL 33mg; IRON 2.3mg; SODIUM 645mg; CALC 315mg

a little more...

Serve yourself a larger portion of soup for a bigger meal. A 1¼-cup serving of soup provides 371 calories.

nutrition note

Butternut Squash

Butternut squash is naturally fat- and cholesterol-free. It's a good source of fiber, potassium, and magnesium, and an excellent source of vitamins A and C.

Gazpacho with Shrimp and Avocado Relish

364 calories

Enjoy a cool summer soup with freshly cooked shrimp and a creamy avocado relish for a quick meal. The shrimp add protein, making this the perfect one-dish lunch. Pair with a warm slice of grilled garlic bread, perfect for dipping, for 114 calories.

SOUP

- 1 pound peeled and deveined large shrimp
- ¾ cup chopped red bell pepper
- ¼ cup chopped fresh cilantro
- 3 tablespoons chopped red onion
- 2 tablespoons fresh lemon juice
- ¾ teaspoon salt
- ½ teaspoon hot pepper sauce
- 1 pound plum tomatoes, seeded and chopped
- 1 medium cucumber, peeled and chopped
- 1 garlic clove
- 1 (11.5-ounce) can low-sodium vegetable juice

RELISH

- ¼ cup finely chopped red bell pepper
- 2 tablespoons chopped fresh cilantro
- 1 tablespoon finely chopped red onion
- 1 teaspoon fresh lemon juice
- 1 ripe peeled avocado, diced

1. To prepare soup, cook shrimp in boiling water 2 minutes or until done. Drain and rinse under cold water; coarsely chop shrimp.

2. Combine ¾ cup bell pepper and next 9 ingredients in a blender; process until smooth. Stir in shrimp.

3. To prepare relish, combine ¼ cup bell pepper and next 4 ingredients. Top soup with relish. **Yield:** 4 servings (serving size: 1 cup soup and about ⅓ cup relish).

CALORIES 250; FAT 9g (sat 1.4g, mono 4.6g, poly 1.7g); PROTEIN 26g; CARB 17.5g; FIBER 6.2g; CHOL 172mg; IRON 3.9mg; SODIUM 675mg; CALC 105mg

Grilled Garlic Bread

- 4 (1-ounce) slices French bread
- 1 tablespoon olive oil
- 1 garlic clove, halved

1. Heat a grill pan over medium-high heat. Brush bread evenly with olive oil. Add bread to pan; cook 1½ minutes on each side. Rub toast with cut sides of garlic; discard garlic. **Yield:** 4 servings (serving size: 1 slice).

CALORIES 112; FAT 3.9g (sat 0.6g, mono 2.6g, poly 0.6g); PROTEIN 3.3g; CARB 16g; FIBER 0.7g; CHOL 0mg; IRON 1.1mg; SODIUM 184mg; CALC 13mg

a little more...

Add a 1-ounce slice of mozzarella to your slice of Grilled Garlic Bread for a cheesier side. It'll add 90 calories to your meal.

nutrition note

Avocado

While avocados may be high in fat, the majority of it is good-for-your-heart unsaturated fat. They're also a good source of fiber, vitamin C, and other nutrients, such as thiamine and riboflavin.

Barley and Beef Soup

Make this soup the night before to allow time for its flavors to develop. Pour hot servings into a thermos to take for lunch, or reheat individual portions in the microwave as needed. Serve with a 1.5-ounce slice of crusty bread (123 calories) to soak up the soup.

Cooking spray
2 cups chopped onion (about 1 large)
1 pound chuck steak, trimmed and cut into ½-inch cubes
1½ cups chopped peeled carrot (about 4)
1 cup chopped celery (about 4 stalks)
5 garlic cloves, minced
1 cup uncooked pearl barley
5 cups fat-free, lower-sodium beef broth
2 cups water
½ cup no-salt-added tomato puree
½ teaspoon kosher salt
¼ teaspoon freshly ground black pepper
2 bay leaves

1. Heat a large Dutch oven over medium heat. Coat pan with cooking spray. Add chopped onion and beef to pan; cook 10 minutes or until onion is tender and beef is browned, stirring occasionally. Add chopped carrot and chopped celery to pan; cook 5 minutes, stirring occasionally. Stir in garlic; cook 30 seconds. Stir in barley and remaining ingredients, and bring to a boil. Cover, reduce heat, and simmer 40 minutes or until barley is done and vegetables are tender. Discard bay leaves. **Yield:** 6 servings (serving size: 1¾ cups).

CALORIES 275; FAT 5g (sat 1.6g, mono 2.3g, poly 0.5g); PROTEIN 21.8g; CARB 36g; 1 8g; CHOL 43mg; IRON 3.1mg; SODIUM 649mg; CALC 57mg

a little more...

For a heartier serving, portion out a 2-cup serving. This slightly larger portion will contain 314 calories.

nutrition note

Lower-Sodium Broth

Purchased broths can harbor lots of sodium, so read the label and choose one that contains 700 milligrams of sodium or less per cup. The easiest way is to pick up a brand labeled lower-sodium. But be aware that some broths, particularly organic brands, contain less sodium but aren't always labeled that way, so read the label closely so you know what you're buying.

Broccoli and Chicken Noodle Soup

396 calories

If the broccoli florets are large, break them into smaller pieces; they'll cook more quickly. Count on having this lunch on the table in about 40 minutes, and serve this soup the moment it's done for the best results. In fact, if you wait, you'll find it gets thicker with time. If you'd like to make it ahead to take for a weekday lunch, you will want to thin the soup with a little chicken broth or milk to the desired consistency. For a crunchy side, serve with wheat crackers—a serving of 6 will add 79 calories.

Cooking spray
- 2 cups chopped onion
- 1 cup presliced mushrooms
- 1 garlic clove, minced
- 3 tablespoons butter
- 1.1 ounces all-purpose flour (about ¼ cup)
- 4 cups 1% low-fat milk
- 1 (14-ounce) can fat-free, lower-sodium chicken broth
- 4 ounces uncooked vermicelli, broken into 2-inch pieces
- 2 cups (8 ounces) shredded light processed cheese (such as Velveeta Light)
- 4 cups (1-inch) cubed cooked chicken breast
- 3 cups small broccoli florets (8 ounces)
- 1 cup half-and-half
- 1 teaspoon freshly ground black pepper
- ¾ teaspoon salt

1. Heat a Dutch oven over medium-high heat. Coat pan with cooking spray. Add onion, mushrooms, and garlic to pan; sauté 5 minutes or until liquid evaporates, stirring occasionally. Reduce heat to medium; add butter to mushroom mixture, stirring until butter melts. Sprinkle mushroom mixture with flour; cook 2 minutes, stirring occasionally. Gradually add milk and broth, stirring constantly with a whisk; bring to a boil. Reduce heat to medium-low; cook 10 minutes or until slightly thick, stirring constantly. Add pasta to pan; cook 10 minutes. Add cheese to pan, and stir until cheese melts. Add chicken and remaining ingredients to pan; cook 5 minutes or until broccoli is tender and soup is thoroughly heated. **Yield:** 10 servings (serving size: 1 cup).

CALORIES 317; FAT 12.3g (sat 6.8g, mono 2.9g poly 0.9g); PROTEIN 27.5g; CARB 23.8g; FIBER 1.9g; CHOL 74mg; IRON 1.6mg; SODIUM 723mg; CALC 179mg

a little more...

This soup makes a lot, so bulk up your meal with a larger portion. A 1¼-cup serving of soup contains 396 calories.

nutrition note

Broccoli

A serving of steamed broccoli offers more than a day's worth of vitamin C, as well as 15 percent of your daily fiber needs, vitamin A, and heart-healthy folate and potassium, all in a low-calorie package.

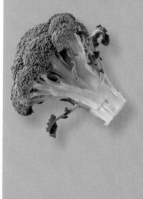

Chili con Carne

A traditional Texas-style chili, this stew packs a smoky punch from mildly spicy poblanos and a hot chipotle chile. Rinsing the chipotle mellows the heat; skip that step for more fire.

360 calories

8 poblano chiles
3 pounds boneless chuck roast, trimmed and cut into ½-inch cubes
1½ teaspoons salt
½ teaspoon black pepper
3 tablespoons all-purpose flour
2 tablespoons olive oil, divided
3 cups chopped onion
4 garlic cloves, minced
3 cups chopped seeded peeled plum tomato (about 10 medium)
1 tablespoon dried oregano
1 tablespoon ground cumin
1 chipotle chile, canned in adobo sauce
3 tablespoons chopped fresh cilantro
6 tablespoons reduced-fat shredded cheddar cheese

1. Preheat broiler.
2. Place poblanos on a foil-lined baking sheet; broil 8 minutes or until charred, turning after 6 minutes. Place poblanos in a zip-top plastic bag; seal. Let stand 15 minutes. Peel and cut chiles into 1-inch pieces.
3. Sprinkle beef with salt and black pepper; dredge in flour. Heat 1 tablespoon olive oil in a Dutch oven over medium-high heat. Add half of beef to pan; sauté 5 minutes, turning to brown on all sides. Remove from pan. Repeat procedure with remaining oil and beef.
4. Reduce heat to medium. Add onion to pan; cook 12 minutes, stirring occasionally. Add garlic; cook 3 minutes, stirring frequently. Return beef to pan. Stir in tomato, oregano, and cumin; bring to a simmer. Cover and cook 1 hour, stirring occasionally. Stir in poblanos; simmer 45 minutes or until beef is tender, stirring occasionally. Rinse, seed, and chop chipotle. Stir in chipotle and cilantro. Sprinkle with cheese. **Yield:** 10 servings (serving size: about 1 cup chili and about 2 teaspoons cheese).

CALORIES 360; FAT 20.9g (sat 7.6g, mono 9.3g, poly 1.1g); PROTEIN 29.2g; CARB 13.8g; FIBER 2.6g; CHOL 84mg; IRON 3.6mg; SODIUM 442mg; CALC 83mg

a little more...

Serve this chili with a side of your favorite cornbread. Recipes vary, but on average, a 2-ounce piece will add about 175 calories to your meal.

nutrition note

Making Healthy Chili

One way to add lots of flavor without lots of calories is using chile peppers in your chili. There are hundreds of options, and each contributes a slightly different flavor, from fruity to bitter, with varying levels of heat. For example, poblanos offer mild heat and a fruity taste. Jalapeños have a sharp, acidic flavor and a medium heat level—if you want to tame the heat, remove the seeds and membranes on the inside walls. Or use serranos to crank up the heat even more.

dinner

- Healthy Ideas for the End of the Day
- Eating Out Tips
- Recipes

dinner

Answering the "what's for dinner" question is something most of us face every night. And while dinner is ideally the moment of the day to wind down and relax, the evening hours can be hurried and rushed and anything but uneventful. While takeout may be an easy solution, it's not always the best idea for those of us who want to watch what we're eating. A better choice is cooking at home, which allows you to control what goes into your dinner so you can monitor calories, fat, and sodium. To help you on those hectic nights when you don't have much time, we've identified recipes that are easier to put together and also those that are better suited for a weekend meal.

Healthy Ideas for the End of the Day

• **Before eating, divide the plate.** Here's a simple rule to portion a plate properly: **Divide it in half. Automatically fill one side with fruits or vegetables, leaving the rest for equal parts protein and starch.** This way, you begin to see what a properly balanced meal looks like.
• **Keep alcohol in check.** A glass of wine, beer, or a mixed drink at the end of the day can be a great way to unwind, and studies have shown that a daily drink can be beneficial to your health. Just one serving of alcohol (a 5-ounce glass of wine, 12 ounces of beer, or 1½ ounces of liquor, spirits, or liqueur) for women and two for men can provide major bang-for-your-buck health benefits. However, moderation is key—an excess amount can undo any benefit alcohol may have provided. If you're pregnant or taking certain medications, you may need to put this healthy habit on hold.

Eating Out Tips

Dining out can be a positive health experience when you choose wisely and avoid overeating. Let the menu be your guide and remember to pay attention to the 3 P's: **portion size, preparation method, and products used.** Watch out for fried foods and those labeled with "red flag" words like butter, cream, and mayonnaise—these menu items are often higher in calories and saturated fat. Sides can be sneaky, too, so request dressing on the side and veggies prepared in olive oil. Consider ordering appetizer-sized portions or ask for half of your meal to be packed in a take-home container before it's brought to the table. If you're not sure about a recipe's ingredients or preparation method, just ask.
• *Grilled Dijon Chicken and Portobellos from Applebee's* = 450 calories
• *Linguine alla Marinara from Olive Garden* = 430 calories
• *Asian Salmon Spinach Salad from Ruby Tuesday* = 494 calories

one side:
fruits and vegetables

one side:
protein and starch

dinner

Fried Catfish with Hush Puppies

479 calories

To balance the plate, add ¾ cup fresh steamed okra (23 calories).

8 cups peanut oil
6 (6-ounce) catfish fillets
½ teaspoon salt
9 ounces all-purpose flour (about 2 cups), divided
1¼ cups cornmeal
1 teaspoon freshly ground black pepper
2 cups buttermilk
2 large eggs
3.4 ounces all-purpose flour (about ¾ cup)
⅓ cup cornmeal
⅓ cup buttermilk
3 tablespoons grated onion
1 teaspoon baking powder
¼ teaspoon salt
¼ teaspoon ground red pepper
1 large egg, lightly beaten
Lemon wedges (optional)

1. To prepare catfish, clip a candy/fry thermometer to a Dutch oven; add oil to pan. Heat oil to 385°.
2. Sprinkle fillets evenly with ½ teaspoon salt. Place 4.5 ounces (1 cup) flour in a shallow dish. Combine remaining 4.5 ounces (1 cup) flour, cornmeal, and black pepper in a shallow dish. Combine 2 cups buttermilk and 2 eggs in a shallow dish. Dredge fillets in flour; dip in buttermilk mixture. Dredge in cornmeal mixture; shake off excess breading. Place 2 fillets in hot oil; cook 5 minutes or until done, turning occasionally. Make sure oil temperature does not drop below 375°. Remove fillets from pan using a slotted spoon; drain on paper towels. Return oil temperature to 385°. Repeat procedure twice with remaining fillets.

3. Weigh or lightly spoon 3.4 ounces (¾ cup) flour into dry measuring cups; level with a knife. Combine 3.4 ounces flour and next 7 ingredients. Drop batter 1 tablespoonful at a time into pan; fry at 375° for 5 minutes or until browned, turning frequently. Remove hush puppies from pan using a slotted spoon; drain on paper towels. Serve with lemon wedges, if desired. **Yield:** 6 servings (serving size: 1 fillet and 2 hush puppies).

CALORIES 456; FAT 18.3g (sat 3.6g, mono 5.4g, poly 7.9g); PROTEIN 29.4g; CARB 42.9g; FIBER 2.6g; CHOL 150mg; IRON 3.6mg; SODIUM 724mg; CALC 170mg

a little more...

Serve with ½ cup of coleslaw (100 calories) and 1 tablespoon of Tartar Sauce (51 calories).

Tartar Sauce

¼ cup organic canola mayonnaise (such as Spectrum)
1 tablespoon dill pickle relish
1 tablespoon chopped fresh flat-leaf parsley
1 teaspoon prepared horseradish
¾ teaspoon fresh lemon juice
⅛ teaspoon salt

1. Combine all ingredients in a small bowl; cover and chill. **Yield:** 8 servings (serving size: 1 tablespoon).

CALORIES 51; FAT 5.5g (sat 0.5g, mono 3g, poly 1.5g); PROTEIN 0g; CARB 0.1g; FIBER 0g; CHOL 3mg; IRON 0mg; SODIUM 122mg; CALC 1mg

nutrition note

Healthier Frying

One key to healthier frying is better batters and breading. Coating foods yields a tasty crust, but breading and batters done wrong can inflate calories and promote oil absorption. All-purpose flour adheres well because it contains gluten, but too much flour causes the food to absorb more oil. Adding gluten-free ingredients like cornmeal reduces oil absorption.

Salmon with Maple-Lemon Glaze

450 calories

Common pantry ingredients create a sweet-tangy glaze for rich salmon fillets. It's also tasty with pork tenderloin or skinless, boneless chicken thighs. Finish the fish under the broiler to caramelize the glaze into a tasty browned crust. Serve with ¾ cup roasted potato wedges (75 calories) and ¾ cup green peas (88 calories).

  2 **tablespoons fresh lemon juice**
  2 **tablespoons maple syrup**
  1 **tablespoon cider vinegar**
  1 **tablespoon canola oil**
  4 **(6-ounce) skinless salmon fillets**
  ½ **teaspoon salt**
  ¼ **teaspoon freshly ground black pepper**
     Cooking spray

1. Preheat broiler.
2. Combine first 4 ingredients in a large zip-top plastic bag. Add fish to bag; seal. Refrigerate 10 minutes, turning bag once.
3. Remove fish from bag, reserving marinade. Place marinade in a microwave-safe bowl. Microwave at HIGH 1 minute.
4. Heat a large ovenproof nonstick skillet over medium-high heat. Sprinkle fish evenly with salt and pepper. Coat pan with cooking spray. Add fish to pan; cook 3 minutes. Turn fish over. Brush marinade evenly over fish. Broil 3 minutes or until fish flakes easily when tested with a fork or until desired degree of doneness.
Yield: 4 servings (serving size: 1 fillet).

CALORIES 287; FAT 14g (sat 2.7g, mono 6.7g, poly 3.6g); PROTEIN 31g; CARB 7.5g; FIBER 0.1g; CHOL 80mg; IRON 0.7mg; SODIUM 363mg; CALC 23mg

a little more...

Instead of the potato wedges, substitute a medium baked potato (110 calories). Top it with 1 tablespoon of shredded cheddar cheese (28 calories), 1 tablespoon of reduced-fat sour cream (20 calories), and 2 teaspoons of chopped fresh chives (less than 1 calorie).

back on track

Focus on Healthful Fats

The best advice regarding fats: Stick with unsaturated fats found in vegetable oils, seeds, nuts, fish, and avocados to promote health and protect against heart disease, stroke, inflammation, and diabetes. Incorporate healthy fats into your day-to-day cooking by cooking veggies in heart-healthy olive or canola oil; incorporating fish, skinless poultry, or lean cuts of beef and pork into your diet; and topping salads with crunchy nuts and seeds instead of buttery croutons.

Fresh Salmon-Cilantro Burgers

414 calories

Spinach Salad with Feta (73 calories per serving), with a sweet, slightly spicy, Asian-influenced dressing, makes a tasty accompaniment.

- ¼ cup reduced-fat mayonnaise
- 1 tablespoon chopped fresh cilantro
- 1 tablespoon fresh lime juice
- ⅛ teaspoon salt
- ⅛ teaspoon black pepper
- 1 (1-pound) salmon fillet, skinned and cut into 1-inch pieces
- ¼ cup dry breadcrumbs
- 2 tablespoons cilantro leaves
- 2 tablespoons chopped green onions
- 2 tablespoons fresh lime juice
- 1 tablespoon chopped seeded jalapeño pepper
- ½ teaspoon salt
- ¼ teaspoon black pepper
- Cooking spray
- 4 (1½-ounce) hamburger buns with sesame seeds, toasted
- 12 (¼-inch-thick) slices English cucumber
- 4 green leaf lettuce leaves

1. Combine first 5 ingredients in a small bowl; cover and chill.
2. Place salmon in a food processor; pulse until coarsely chopped. Add breadcrumbs and next 6 ingredients; pulse 4 times or until well blended. Divide salmon mixture into 4 equal portions, shaping each into a ¾-inch-thick patty.
3. Heat a grill pan over medium-high heat. Coat pan with cooking spray. Add patties to pan; cook 2 minutes. Carefully turn patties over, and cook 2 minutes or until done.

4. Spread about 1 tablespoon mayonnaise mixture over bottom half of each hamburger bun. Top each serving with 1 salmon patty, 3 cucumber slices, 1 lettuce leaf, and top half of bun. **Yield:** 4 servings (serving size: 1 burger).

CALORIES 341; FAT 11.5g (sat 2g, mono 2.9g, poly 4.9g); PROTEIN 31.6g; CARB 30.9g; FIBER 1.8g; CHOL 66mg; IRON 2.2mg; SODIUM 816mg; CALC 67mg

Spinach Salad with Feta

- 2 tablespoons hoisin sauce
- 1 tablespoon rice vinegar
- 2 teaspoons canola oil
- 2 teaspoons water
- ¼ teaspoon chile paste
- ½ (5-ounce) package baby spinach
- ½ cup yellow bell pepper strips
- ¼ cup thinly sliced red onion
- ¼ cup (1 ounce) crumbled feta cheese

1. Combine first 5 ingredients in a large bowl; stir well with a whisk. Add spinach and remaining ingredients to bowl; toss to coat. **Yield:** 4 servings.

CALORIES 73; FAT 4.6g (sat 1.6g, mono 1.9g, poly 0.9g); PROTEIN 2.2g; CARB 6g; FIBER 1g; CHOL 9mg; IRON 0.8mg; SODIUM 256mg; CALC 68mg

a little more...

Sweet potato fries would make a tasty side. A serving of 20 fries will provide 250 calories.

nutrition note

Salmon

Salmon is a fatty fish, but it's loaded with heart-healthy omega-3 fatty acids. These healthful polyunsaturated fats help improve cardiovascular health by controlling cholesterol and reducing blood pressure.

Roasted Tilapia with Orange-Parsley Salsa

451 calories

All parts of the orange—juice, rind, and pulp—flavor the quickly cooked fish. Substitute brown, basmati, or jasmine rice, if you prefer. Round out your plate with a side of steamed asparagus. You'll need about 1 pound of asparagus to serve four people—each serving will add 28 calories to this meal.

- 3 **oranges (about 1 pound)**
- ¼ **cup chopped fresh parsley, divided**
- 2 **tablespoons extra-virgin olive oil, divided**
- ¾ **teaspoon salt, divided**
- 4 **(6-ounce) tilapia fillets**
- ½ **teaspoon freshly ground black pepper, divided**
- 2 **cups hot cooked instant white rice**

1. Preheat oven to 400°.

2. Grate 2 teaspoons orange rind. Peel and section oranges over a bowl, reserving 2 tablespoons juice. Chop sections. Combine rind, chopped orange, 2 tablespoons parsley, 5 teaspoons oil, and ¼ teaspoon salt in a bowl; toss well.

3. Sprinkle fish evenly with ¼ teaspoon salt and ¼ teaspoon pepper. Place fish in an ovenproof skillet coated with remaining 1 teaspoon oil. Bake at 400° for 14 minutes or until fish flakes easily when tested with a fork or until desired degree of doneness.

4. Combine 2 tablespoons reserved juice, remaining 2 tablespoons parsley, remaining ¼ teaspoon salt, remaining ¼ teaspoon pepper, and rice. Spoon ½ cup rice onto each of 4 plates; top each with 1 fillet and ¼ cup salsa. **Yield:** 4 servings.

CALORIES 423; FAT 12.1g (sat 2.6g, mono 6.7g, poly 2.1g); PROTEIN 47.4g; CARB 32.7g; FIBER 3g; CHOL 97mg; IRON 3mg; SODIUM 543mg; CALC 76mg

a little more...

For a citrusy addition, serve with half a grapefruit, which will add 60 calories. To cut the bitterness some, you can sprinkle your half with 1 teaspoon sugar—that'll add 16 calories to your meal.

back on track

Use Your Power for Good

Most homes have a nutritional "gatekeeper" who controls 72 percent of the food eaten by everyone else. The person who chooses food, buys it, and prepares it wields power. If that's you, take advantage of it. If not, get more involved in the food choices of your household.

Tilapia Tostadas with Roasted Corn Relish

These crisp tostadas have all the appeal of fish tacos, but the flat shape allows you to pile toppings high. Although we broil corn tortillas for the base, substitute flour tortillas, or use prepared shells, if you prefer.

½ cup reduced-fat sour cream
¼ cup green salsa
Cooking spray
1 cup yellow corn kernels
¼ cup finely chopped red bell pepper
¼ cup finely chopped red onion
1½ teaspoons minced seeded jalapeño pepper
¾ teaspoon salt, divided
1 cup diced peeled avocado
2 teaspoons fresh lime juice
1½ pounds tilapia fillets, cut into 2-inch pieces
¼ teaspoon freshly ground black pepper
⅓ cup yellow cornmeal
1 tablespoon canola oil, divided
8 (6-inch) corn tortillas
1 cup packaged angel hair slaw
Lime wedges (optional)

1. Combine sour cream and salsa.
2. Heat a large nonstick skillet over medium-high heat. Coat pan with cooking spray. Add corn, bell pepper, onion, jalapeño, and ¼ teaspoon salt to pan; sauté 5 minutes, stirring occasionally. Remove mixture from pan; wipe pan clean with paper towels. Combine avocado and juice; toss gently. Stir avocado mixture into corn mixture.
3. Preheat broiler.
4. Sprinkle fish evenly with remaining ½ teaspoon salt and black pepper. Place cornmeal in a shallow dish; dredge fish in cornmeal. Heat 1½ teaspoons oil in pan over medium-high heat. Add half of fish to pan; cook 3 minutes. Carefully turn fish over; cook 2 minutes or until fish flakes easily when tested with a fork or until desired degree of doneness. Repeat procedure with remaining 1½ teaspoons oil and fish.
5. Coat both sides of tortillas with cooking spray. Arrange tortillas in a single layer on baking sheets; broil 2 minutes on each side or until crisp. Place 2 tortillas on each of 4 plates. Arrange 2 tablespoons slaw on each tortilla. Divide fish evenly among tortillas; top each serving with about 3 tablespoons corn relish and about 1½ tablespoons sour cream mixture. Serve with lime wedges, if desired.
Yield: 4 servings.

CALORIES 470; FAT 17.1g (sat 4.3g, mono 7.6g, poly 3.3g); PROTEIN 40.4g; CARB 43.7g; FIBER 6.7g; CHOL 96mg; IRON 2.2mg; SODIUM 610mg; CALC 83mg

a little more...

Serve this with a side of chips and salsa. A ½-cup serving of fresh salsa and a serving of 15 light baked tortilla chips (a little less than an ounce total) will add 155 calories to this meal.

nutrition note

Corn Tortillas

A standard 6-inch corn tortilla contains about half the fat and calories and one-fourth the sodium of a similar-sized flour tortilla.

Tuna Noodle Casserole

Although the recipe calls for egg noodles, you can use any short pasta to make this dish.

8 ounces wide egg noodles
2 tablespoons olive oil
½ cup chopped yellow onion
⅓ cup chopped carrot
2 tablespoons all-purpose flour
2¾ cups fat-free milk
½ cup (4 ounces) ⅓-less-fat cream cheese, softened
2 tablespoons Dijon mustard
½ teaspoon salt
½ teaspoon freshly ground black pepper
1 cup frozen peas, thawed
½ cup (2 ounces) grated Parmigiano-Reggiano cheese, divided
2 (5-ounce) cans albacore tuna in water, drained and flaked
Cooking spray

1. Preheat broiler.
2. Cook noodles according to package directions, omitting salt and fat. Drain. Heat a large skillet over medium heat. Add oil to pan; swirl to coat. Add onion and carrot; cook 6 minutes or until carrot is almost tender, stirring occasionally. Sprinkle with flour; cook 1 minute, stirring constantly. Gradually stir in milk; cook 5 minutes, stirring constantly with a whisk until slightly thick. Stir in cream cheese, mustard, salt, and pepper; cook 2 minutes, stirring constantly.
3. Remove pan from heat. Stir in noodles, peas, ¼ cup Parmigiano-Reggiano cheese, and tuna. Spoon mixture into a shallow broiler-safe 2-quart baking dish coated with cooking spray; top with remaining ¼ cup Parmigiano-Reggiano cheese. Broil 3 minutes or until golden and bubbly. Let stand 5 minutes before serving. **Yield:** 6 servings (serving size: 1⅓ cups).

CALORIES 422; FAT 16.5g (sat 7.1g, mono 6.3g, poly 1.8g); PROTEIN 27.4g; CARB 40.6g; FIBER 3g; CHOL 88mg; IRON 2.4mg; SODIUM 756mg; CALC 293mg

a little more…

Serve yourself a larger portion of this classic dish made light. A 1½-cup serving will provide 475 calories.

nutrition note

Egg Noodles

Egg noodles are wheat noodles made with egg—the egg adds flavor, color, and texture. You'll also find yolk-free (or no yolk) options in the grocery store. This variety contains less saturated fat than egg noodles with the yolks. You can also increase the nutritional ante by choosing whole-wheat egg noodles.

Crab Cakes with Roasted Vegetables and Tangy Butter Sauce

443 calories

- ¼ cup finely chopped red onion
- 2 tablespoons chopped fresh parsley
- 3 tablespoons light mayonnaise
- 2 teaspoons Dijon mustard
- ¾ teaspoon Old Bay seasoning
- ½ teaspoon Worcestershire sauce
- 2 large egg whites, lightly beaten
- 1 pound lump crabmeat, drained and shell pieces removed
- 1½ cups panko (Japanese breadcrumbs), divided
- 1 tablespoon olive oil, divided
- Cooking spray
- 21 baby carrots (about 12 ounces)
- 5 small red potatoes, quartered (about 8 ounces)
- 4 medium shallots, halved lengthwise
- ⅛ teaspoon salt
- 8 ounces haricots verts, trimmed
- ⅔ cup fat-free, lower-sodium chicken broth
- 3 tablespoons chopped shallots
- 2 tablespoons white wine vinegar
- 2½ tablespoons butter

1. Combine first 7 ingredients in a medium bowl. Gently fold in crabmeat. Gently stir in ¾ cup panko. Cover and chill 30 minutes.
2. Preheat oven to 450°.
3. Divide crab mixture into 8 equal portions (about ½ cup each); shape each into a ¾-inch-thick patty. Place remaining ¾ cup panko in a shallow dish. Working with 1 patty at a time, dredge in panko. Repeat procedure with remaining patties and panko.

4. Heat 1½ teaspoons oil in a medium nonstick skillet over medium heat. Coat both sides of crab cakes with cooking spray. Add 4 crab cakes to pan; cook 7 minutes. Carefully turn cakes over; cook 7 minutes or until golden. Repeat procedure with remaining 1½ teaspoons oil, remaining 4 crab cakes, and cooking spray.
5. Leave root and 1-inch stem on carrots; scrub with a brush. Combine carrots, potatoes, and shallots in a small roasting pan. Coat vegetables with cooking spray; sprinkle with ⅛ teaspoon salt. Toss. Bake at 450° for 20 minutes, turning once. Coat haricots verts with cooking spray. Add haricots verts to vegetable mixture; toss. Bake an additional 10 minutes or until vegetables are tender.
6. Combine broth, shallots, and vinegar in a small saucepan; bring to a boil. Cook until reduced to ¼ cup (about 4 minutes); remove from heat. Stir in butter. Serve with crab cakes and vegetables. **Yield:** 4 servings (serving size: 2 crab cakes, about 1 cup vegetables, and about 1½ tablespoons sauce).

CALORIES 443; FAT 16.7g (sat 5.6g, mono 5.2g, poly 2.9g); PROTEIN 32.8g; CARB 42g; FIBER 7g; CHOL 103mg; IRON 2mg; SODIUM 969mg; CALC 163mg

a little more...

Pair these crab cakes with a crisp white wine. A 5-ounce glass will add about 120 calories to your meal.

nutrition note

A Lighter Crab Cake

Instead of being light and refreshing, many crab cakes are heavy in calories, sodium, and saturated fat. Plus, they're often loaded with high-calorie and sodium-laden fillers and then deep-fried. For a lighter version, we lightly season sweet, premium crab with just enough mayonnaise, Dijon mustard, egg whites, and panko (Japanese breadcrumbs) to bind it all together. The cakes are cooked in a small amount of oil instead of deep-fried.

Seared Scallops with Warm Tuscan Beans

426 calories

Pair this one-dish meal with a side of Grilled Garlic Bread—a serving will add 112 calories to the meal. It's perfect for sopping up every last drop of the delicious sauce.

2 tablespoons olive oil, divided
1½ pounds sea scallops
¼ teaspoon salt
1 cup prechopped onion
⅛ teaspoon crushed red pepper
2 garlic cloves, minced
¼ cup dry white wine
1 cup fat-free, lower-sodium chicken broth
1 (19-ounce) can cannellini beans or other white beans, rinsed and drained
1 (6-ounce) package fresh baby spinach
2 tablespoons chopped fresh basil

1. Heat 1 tablespoon oil in a large non-stick skillet over medium-high heat. Sprinkle scallops evenly with salt. Add scallops to pan; cook 2 minutes on each side or until done. Remove scallops from pan; keep warm.
2. Add remaining 1 tablespoon oil and onion to pan; sauté 2 minutes. Add pepper and garlic; cook 20 seconds, stirring constantly. Stir in wine; cook 1 minute or until most of liquid evaporates. Stir in broth and beans; cook 2 minutes. Add spinach; cook 1 minute or until spinach wilts. Remove from heat; stir in basil. **Yield:** 4 servings (serving size: about 4 ounces scallops and ¾ cup bean mixture).

CALORIES 314; FAT 8.7g (sat 1.2g, mono 5.1g, poly 1.8g); PROTEIN 33.7g; CARB 24.8g; FIBER 6.1g; CHOL 56mg; IRON 3.2mg; SODIUM 781mg; CALC 112mg

Grilled Garlic Bread

1 tablespoon olive oil
4 (1-ounce) slices French bread
1 garlic clove, halved

1. Heat a grill pan over medium heat. Brush oil evenly over bread slices. Add bread to pan; cook 2 minutes on each side or until lightly browned. Rub 1 side of each bread slice with cut sides of a halved garlic clove. Discard garlic. **Yield:** 4 servings (serving size: 1 slice).

CALORIES 112; FAT 3.9g (sat 0.6g, mono 2.6g, poly 0.6g); PROTEIN 3.3g; CARB 16g; FIBER 0.7g; CHOL 0mg; IRON 1.1mg; SODIUM 184mg; CALC 13mg

a little more...

Serve your garlic bread with a small dish of olive oil for dipping—1 tablespoon of oil will add 120 calories.

nutrition note

Scallops

When buying scallops, bypass the "wet packed" variety and opt for "dry packed" instead. Wet packed scallops have been treated with a liquid solution that contains added sodium. The scallops absorb this salty mixture and plump up, resulting in a heavier weight and a higher market price. But when you cook them, the liquid in these plump scallops cooks out, leaving you with smaller scallops and a higher sodium content.

Shrimp Fra Diavolo

477 calories

Shrimp Fra Diavolo recipes can often be very hot, but you can add or take away the spice by adding more or less red pepper depending on your personal preference. Be sure to use inexpensive medium-sized shrimp in this garlicky, spicy classic.

- 8 **ounces uncooked linguine**
- 2 **tablespoons extra-virgin olive oil, divided**
- 1½ **tablespoons minced garlic, divided**
- 1 **pound medium shrimp, peeled and deveined**
- ¾ **cup diced onion**
- 1 **teaspoon crushed red pepper**
- ½ **teaspoon dried basil**
- ½ **teaspoon dried oregano**
- 2 **tablespoons tomato paste**
- 1 **tablespoon fresh lemon juice**
- 1¾ **cups canned crushed tomatoes**
- 1 **(14.5-ounce) can diced tomatoes, drained**
- ¼ **teaspoon salt**

1. Cook pasta according to package directions, omitting salt and fat. Drain; keep warm.

2. While pasta cooks, heat 1 tablespoon oil in a large nonstick skillet over medium-high heat. Add 1½ teaspoons garlic and shrimp; sauté 3 minutes or until shrimp are done. Remove from pan; keep warm.

3. Add remaining 1 tablespoon oil and onion to pan; sauté 5 minutes or until softened. Stir in remaining 1 tablespoon garlic, pepper, basil, and oregano; cook 1 minute, stirring constantly. Stir in tomato paste and lemon juice; cook 1 minute or until slightly darkened. Stir in crushed tomatoes, diced tomatoes, and salt; cook 5 minutes or until thickened. Return shrimp to pan; cook 2 minutes or until thoroughly heated. Serve over pasta.

Yield: 4 servings (serving size: 1 cup pasta and about 1¼ cups sauce).

CALORIES 477; FAT 10.7g (sat 1.4g, mono 5.3g, poly 1.7g); PROTEIN 33g; CARB 59.4g; FIBER 5.4g; CHOL 172mg; IRON 5.4mg; SODIUM 552mg; CALC 121mg

a little more...

Serve a 1½-ounce piece of French bread with this tasty pasta. It'll provide 123 calories and help you get every last bit of the sauce.

back on track

Head Off the Mindless Munch

Five minutes after eating at an Italian restaurant, 31 percent of people couldn't remember how much bread they ate. If you're worried you might do the same (at a restaurant or at home), serve yourself a portion of the bread and remove the rest from the table.

Greek Shrimp and Asparagus Risotto

480 calories

Sweet onion, rich feta cheese, and fresh dill provide dynamic flavor in this easy weeknight meal. Balance the plate with Quick Fennel Salad, which provides 54 calories per serving.

- **3** cups fat-free, lower-sodium chicken broth
- **1** cup water
- **2** teaspoons olive oil
- **2¾** cups chopped Vidalia or other sweet onion (about 2 medium)
- **1** cup Arborio rice
- **2** garlic cloves, minced
- **1¾** cups (½-inch) sliced asparagus (about 8 ounces)
- **1** pound peeled and deveined medium shrimp, cut into 1-inch pieces
- **½** cup (2 ounces) crumbled feta cheese
- **1** tablespoon chopped fresh dill
- **2** tablespoons fresh lemon juice
- **¼** teaspoon salt
- **⅛** teaspoon freshly ground black pepper

1. Bring broth and 1 cup water to a simmer in a medium saucepan (do not boil). Keep warm over low heat.
2. Heat oil in a large saucepan over medium-high heat. Add onion to pan; sauté 5 minutes or until tender. Stir in rice and garlic; sauté 1 minute. Add broth mixture, ½ cup at a time, stirring constantly until each portion of broth is absorbed before adding the next (about 30 minutes total).

3. Stir in asparagus and shrimp; cook 5 minutes or until shrimp are done, stirring constantly. Remove from heat; stir in cheese and remaining ingredients. **Yield:** 4 servings (serving size: 1½ cups).

CALORIES 426; FAT 8.9g (sat 3.6g, mono 2.8g, poly 1.2g); PROTEIN 33g; CARB 53.5g; FIBER 5.1g; CHOL 189mg; IRON 4.5mg; SODIUM 868mg; CALC 194mg

Quick Fennel Salad

- **2** tablespoons fresh lemon juice
- **1** tablespoon olive oil
- **¼** teaspoon salt
- **¼** teaspoon crushed fennel seeds
- **⅛** teaspoon freshly ground black pepper
- **6** cups torn romaine lettuce
- **1** cup thinly sliced fennel bulb

1. Combine first 5 ingredients in a large bowl. Add lettuce and fennel; toss well to coat. **Yield:** 4 servings.

CALORIES 54; FAT 3.7g (sat 0.5g, mono 2.5g, poly 0.5g); PROTEIN 1.4g; CARB 5.1g; FIBER 2.5g; CHOL 0mg; IRON 1mg; SODIUM 164mg; CALC 41mg

a little more...

For a sweet side, pair this meal with a cup of fresh grapes. It'll add 120 calories.

quick fix

Daily Activities

Don't discount the movement you do as part of your daily life. An hour spent mowing the lawn can burn more than 350 calories (assuming you don't spend it seated on a riding lawn mower), while an hour spent raking the lawn can burn over 250 calories. Even general house cleaning can burn 200 calories an hour.

Smothered Steak Burgers

488 calories

Sautéed mushrooms, steak sauce, and Worcestershire sauce create robust flavors in this knife-and-fork burger. Serve with a side of baked oven fries. A 2-ounce serving of fries (such as Alexia) will add 90 calories to your meal.

Cooking spray
2   tablespoons finely chopped shallots
1   garlic clove, minced
1   (8-ounce) package presliced button mushrooms
½   cup fat-free, lower-sodium beef broth
1   tablespoon lower-sodium steak sauce (such as Angostura)
1   teaspoon cornstarch
½   teaspoon freshly ground black pepper, divided
2   tablespoons ketchup
1   tablespoon Worcestershire sauce
1   pound ground sirloin
¼   teaspoon salt
4   green leaf lettuce leaves
4   (½-inch-thick) slices tomato
4   (2-ounce) Kaiser rolls, toasted

1. Heat a large nonstick skillet over medium heat. Coat pan with cooking spray. Add shallots and garlic to pan; cook 1 minute or until tender, stirring frequently. Increase heat to medium-high. Add mushrooms to pan; cook 10 minutes or until moisture evaporates, stirring occasionally. Combine broth, steak sauce, and cornstarch, stirring with a whisk. Add broth mixture to pan; bring to a boil. Cook 1 minute or until thickened, stirring constantly. Stir in ¼ teaspoon pepper. Remove mushroom mixture from pan; cover and keep warm. Wipe pan with paper towels.
2. Combine remaining ¼ teaspoon pepper, ketchup, and Worcestershire sauce in a large bowl, stirring with a whisk. Add beef to bowl; toss gently to combine. Shape beef mixture into 4 (½-inch-thick) patties; sprinkle evenly with salt.
3. Heat pan over medium-high heat. Coat pan with cooking spray. Add patties to pan; cook 4 minutes. Turn and cook 3 minutes or until desired degree of doneness. Place 1 lettuce leaf and 1 tomato slice on the bottom half of each roll. Top each serving with 1 patty, about ¼ cup mushroom mixture, and top half of roll.
Yield: 4 servings (serving size: 1 burger).

CALORIES 398; FAT 12.9g (sat 4.4g, mono 5.1g, poly 1.4g); PROTEIN 30.7g; CARB 38.4g; FIBER 1.9g; CHOL 41mg; IRON 4.9mg; SODIUM 747mg; CALC 79mg

a little more...

Pair with an ice-cold beer. Depending on the type of beer you choose, a 12-ounce glass will add about 150 calories.

quick fix

Turn Off the Television

The vast wasteland that is TV-land leads to vast waists. It's not just the couch-sitting. TV distracts you from how much you're eating, and the more you watch, the more you're likely to eat. In a study comparing how much popcorn viewers ate during a half-hour show or an hour-long show, those who watched more television ate 28 percent more popcorn.

Beef Tenderloin Steaks with Shiitake Mushroom Sauce

The steaks are sautéed in cooking spray to create a crust, while the mushrooms are sautéed in butter for flavor. Since the mushrooms release liquid as they cook, the butter is less likely to burn. Shiitake mushrooms create a sublime sauce with deep, earthy flavor, but you can substitute any other mushroom variety. Serve with ½ cup of mashed potatoes (127 calories) and 3 stalks of fresh steamed broccolini (13 calories).

4 (4-ounce) beef tenderloin steaks (1 inch thick), trimmed
½ teaspoon salt, divided
¼ teaspoon freshly ground black pepper, divided
Cooking spray
2 teaspoons butter
2 garlic cloves, minced
4 cups thinly sliced shiitake mushroom caps (about 8 ounces)
½ teaspoon chopped fresh thyme
2 tablespoons balsamic vinegar
1 tablespoon water
1 teaspoon lower-sodium soy sauce
1 tablespoon fresh thyme leaves

1. Sprinkle steaks with ¼ teaspoon salt and ⅛ teaspoon pepper. Heat a large nonstick skillet over medium-high heat. Coat pan with cooking spray. Add steaks to pan; sauté 3 minutes on each side or until desired degree of doneness. Transfer steaks to a serving platter.

2. Heat pan over medium-high heat. Add butter to pan, swirling to coat; cook 15 seconds or until foam subsides. Add garlic to pan; sauté 30 seconds, stirring constantly. Add mushrooms, ½ teaspoon chopped thyme, remaining ¼ teaspoon salt, and remaining ⅛ teaspoon pepper to pan; sauté 3 minutes or until mushrooms are tender, stirring frequently. Stir in vinegar, 1 tablespoon water, and soy sauce; cook 1 minute or until liquid almost evaporates. Spoon mushroom mixture over steaks. Sprinkle with thyme leaves. **Yield:** 4 servings (serving size: 1 steak, ¼ cup mushroom mixture, and ¾ teaspoon thyme leaves).

CALORIES 326; FAT 11.2g (sat 4.7g, mono 4.2g, poly 0.5g); PROTEIN 34.9g; CARB 22.9g; FIBER 3.2g; CHOL 95mg; IRON 2.9mg; SODIUM 428mg; CALC 34mg

a little more...

For a sweet but healthy side, add a cup of diced fresh pineapple for an additional 74 calories.

quick fix

Winter Activity

In the heart of winter, some people are more inclined to be sedentary, but you can stave off cabin fever and stay healthy by bundling up for outdoor activities. In 30 minutes, you can burn more than 200 calories ice skating or shoveling snow and more than 150 by having a snowball fight or making snow angels.

dinner

Flank Steak with Roasted Endive, Spring Onion Agrodolce, and Arugula

½ cup honey
12 ounces spring onions, trimmed and quartered
½ cup sherry vinegar
2 tablespoons olive oil, divided
6 heads Belgian endive (about 1 pound), halved lengthwise
¾ teaspoon salt, divided
¾ teaspoon freshly ground black pepper, divided
2 tablespoons chopped fresh oregano, divided
1½ teaspoons Hungarian sweet paprika
1 (1-pound) flank steak, halved crosswise
6 cups arugula leaves (about 4 ounces)
2 tablespoons extra-virgin olive oil
1 tablespoon fresh lemon juice

1. Place honey in a medium saucepan over medium heat; cook 2 minutes or until heated. Add onions to pan; stir to combine. Stir in vinegar; bring to a boil. Cover, reduce heat, and simmer 30 minutes or until onions are tender. Cook, uncovered, 20 minutes or until syrupy.
2. Preheat oven to 375°.
3. Heat an ovenproof grill pan over medium-high heat. Add 1 tablespoon oil to pan, swirling to coat. Sprinkle endive evenly with ¼ teaspoon salt and ¼ teaspoon black pepper. Add endive, cut sides down, to pan. Cook 1 minute or until lightly browned. Turn endive; place pan in oven. Bake at 375° for 15 minutes or until endive is tender. Remove endive from oven; cover and keep warm. Wipe pan clean.
4. Combine remaining ½ teaspoon salt, remaining ½ teaspoon pepper, 1 tablespoon oregano, and paprika in a small bowl. Sprinkle beef evenly with oregano mixture. Heat grill pan over medium-high heat. Add remaining 1 tablespoon oil to pan, swirling to coat. Add beef to pan; cook 4 minutes on each side or until desired degree of doneness. Let stand 10 minutes before cutting across the grain into thin slices.
5. Combine remaining 1 tablespoon oregano, arugula, 2 tablespoons oil, and juice in a medium bowl; toss gently. Serve steak with endive and arugula salad; top steak with onion mixture. **Yield:** 4 servings (serving size: about 3 ounces steak, about 1 cup salad, 3 endive halves, and about 5 tablespoons onion mixture).

CALORIES 484; FAT 19.9g (sat 4.3g, mono 12.5g, poly 1.7g); PROTEIN 27.4g; CARB 49.5g; FIBER 5.3g; CHOL 37mg; IRON 3mg; SODIUM 505mg; CALC 120mg

a little more...
Pair this meal with a 1½-ounce slice of Italian bread. It'll add 115 calories.

nutrition note

Spring Onions

A spring onion is an onion that's been harvested while still immature, with a small bulb and leaves attached. The regular consumption of onions has been shown to lower cholesterol and blood pressure, both of which help prevent atherosclerosis and diabetes, and reduce the risk of stroke or heart attack.

Ancho Chile–Beef Fajitas with Mango

Ground ancho chiles add subtle, earthy heat. If you prefer more spice, substitute chipotle chile powder.

1 teaspoon fresh lime juice
¾ teaspoon ground ancho chile powder
½ teaspoon Worcestershire sauce
¼ teaspoon ground cumin
1 (8-ounce) beef tenderloin, trimmed and cut into ¼-inch-thick strips
1 teaspoon olive oil
½ cup thinly sliced sweet onion
½ cup thinly sliced red bell pepper
½ cup thinly sliced green bell pepper
½ cup thinly sliced mango
1 plum tomato, coarsely chopped
2 teaspoons lower-sodium soy sauce
1 tablespoon chopped fresh cilantro
4 (6-inch) fat-free flour tortillas
2 tablespoons prepared salsa
2 tablespoons reduced-fat sour cream

1. Combine lime juice, chile powder, Worcestershire sauce, and cumin in a medium bowl. Add beef; toss well.
2. Heat oil in a large nonstick skillet over medium-high heat. Add onion and bell pepper to pan; sauté 4 minutes or until onion is almost tender, stirring occasionally. Add mango and tomato to pan; sauté 1 minute. Add beef mixture; sauté 2 minutes or until desired degree of doneness, stirring occasionally. Add soy sauce; cook 15 seconds. Remove from heat; stir in cilantro.

3. Heat tortillas according to package directions. Place 2 tortillas on each of 2 plates; top each tortilla with about ¾ cup beef mixture. Top each tortilla with 1½ teaspoons prepared salsa and 1½ teaspoons sour cream. **Yield:** 2 servings.

CALORIES 450; FAT 12.9g (sat 3.9g, mono 4.7g, poly 0.7g); PROTEIN 30.6g; CARB 54.6g; FIBER 5.2g; CHOL 68mg; IRON 2.3mg; SODIUM 930mg; CALC 86mg

a little more...

Pair this with Easy Guacamole (94 calories) and a serving of 15 light baked tortilla chips (155 calories) as a side dish.

Easy Guacamole

¾ cup chopped avocado
1 tablespoon finely chopped red onion
2 teaspoons chopped fresh cilantro
1½ teaspoons fresh lemon juice
¼ teaspoon salt
⅛ teaspoon ground red pepper

1. Combine all ingredients in a bowl, and mash to desired consistency. Serve immediately with baked tortilla chips. **Yield:** 2 servings.

CALORIES 94; FAT 8.6g (sat 1.4g, mono 5.4g, poly 1.1g); PROTEIN 1.2g; CARB 5g; FIBER 3g; CHOL 0mg; IRON 0.6mg; SODIUM 297mg; CALC 8mg

quick
fix

Racquetball

A 30-minute game of racquetball can burn about 250 calories. Plus, it's a great way to spend time with a friend or your children.

Curried Beef Short Ribs

422 calories

Finishing this dish with lime zest and juice brightens its rich flavors. Serve with steamed baby bok choy to round out your meal. Four baby bok choy (about 1 pound) should be enough to serve four—one serving will add 12 calories to your meal.

2 teaspoons canola oil
2 pounds beef short ribs, trimmed
1½ teaspoons kosher salt, divided
¼ teaspoon freshly ground black pepper, divided
⅓ cup minced shallots
3 tablespoons minced garlic
3 tablespoons minced peeled fresh ginger
¼ cup water
2 tablespoons red curry paste
¼ cup light coconut milk
1 tablespoon sugar
1 tablespoon fish sauce
1 teaspoon grated lime rind
1 tablespoon fresh lime juice
4 cups hot cooked basmati rice

1. Heat oil in a large nonstick skillet over medium-high heat. Sprinkle ribs with ¾ teaspoon salt and ⅛ teaspoon pepper. Add half of ribs to pan; cook 2 minutes on each side or until browned. Place ribs in an electric slow cooker. Repeat procedure with remaining ribs.
2. Add shallots, garlic, and ginger to pan; sauté 2 minutes. Stir in ¼ cup water and curry paste; cook 1 minute. Stir in coconut milk, sugar, and fish sauce. Add coconut milk mixture to cooker. Cover and cook on LOW 6 hours.
3. Remove ribs from cooker; keep warm. Strain cooking liquid through a colander over a bowl; discard solids. Place a zip-top plastic bag inside a 2-cup glass measure. Pour cooking liquid into bag; let stand 10 minutes (fat will rise to the top). Seal bag; carefully snip off 1 bottom corner of bag. Drain drippings into a small bowl, stopping before fat layer reaches opening; discard fat. Stir in remaining ¾ teaspoon salt, remaining ⅛ teaspoon pepper, rind, and juice. Shred rib meat with 2 forks; discard bones. Serve sauce over ribs and rice. **Yield:** 6 servings (serving size: about 3 ounces ribs, ⅔ cup rice, and about 2½ tablespoons sauce).

CALORIES 410; FAT 16.1g (sat 6.5g, mono 7g, poly 0.9g); PROTEIN 27g; CARB 37.1g; FIBER 0.7g; CHOL 70mg; IRON 4.1mg; SODIUM 841mg; CALC 24mg

a little more...

Pair this meal with a calcium-rich glass of milk—milk with dinner isn't just for kids. A cup of fat-free milk will add 90 calories and about 300 milligrams of calcium (about a third of your daily needs).

nutrition note

Curry Paste

Often used in Thai cuisine, curry paste is a blend of ground herbs, spices, and seasonings. It's intensely flavorful and is a way to add loads of taste without adding many calories—1 tablespoon contains 10 calories. But be aware, this paste also brings a hefty dose of sodium with it—anywhere from 250 to more than 500 milligrams per tablespoon. The good news is that a little goes a long way.

Lamb Chops with Olive Couscous

480 calories

This recipe is quick, easy, and delicious and it would also make a spectacular meal for guests.

- 1 tablespoon dried oregano
- 2 tablespoons extra-virgin olive oil
- ½ teaspoon black pepper
- 3 garlic cloves, minced
- 8 (4-ounce) lamb loin chops, trimmed
- ½ teaspoon salt
- Cooking spray
- 1 (14-ounce) can fat-free, lower-sodium chicken broth
- 1 cup uncooked couscous
- ½ cup cherry tomatoes, halved
- ¼ cup chopped pitted kalamata olives
- 3 tablespoons crumbled feta cheese

1. Preheat broiler.
2. Combine first 4 ingredients. Sprinkle lamb with salt; rub with 1 tablespoon oil mixture. Place on a broiler pan coated with cooking spray. Broil 4 minutes on each side or until done.
3. While lamb cooks, heat a medium saucepan over medium-high heat. Add remaining oil mixture; cook 20 seconds, stirring constantly. Stir in broth; bring to a boil. Stir in couscous. Remove from heat; cover and let stand 5 minutes. Fluff with a fork. Stir in tomatoes, olives, and cheese. Serve couscous mixture with lamb. **Yield:** 4 servings (serving size: 2 lamb chops and 1¼ cups couscous mixture).

CALORIES 480; FAT 19.8g (sat 5.6g, mono 10.8g, poly 1.7g); PROTEIN 36.2g; CARB 36.8g; FIBER 3g; CHOL 97mg; IRON 3.3mg; SODIUM 793mg; CALC 90mg

a little more...

Balance this plate with an ear of fresh corn. One medium ear will add 90 calories.

nutrition note

Lamb

This young, tender cut of meat offers a lean source of protein. The leanest cuts will be labeled "loin" or "leg" on the package. Some lean cuts include leg loin, chops, arm chops, and foreshanks. Ground lamb is also fairly lean and can be used in the same way as ground beef.

Farfalle with Lamb Ragù, Ricotta, and Mint

A classic flavor combination, lamb and mint meet bow-tie pasta for a hearty weeknight meal.

4 teaspoons extra-virgin olive oil, divided
8 ounces lean ground lamb
¾ teaspoon kosher salt, divided
½ cup finely chopped onion
¼ cup finely chopped carrot
1 teaspoon minced fresh rosemary
2 garlic cloves, minced
½ cup dry white wine
⅛ teaspoon freshly ground black pepper
1½ cups canned crushed tomatoes, undrained
½ cup fat-free, lower-sodium chicken broth
8 ounces uncooked farfalle (bow-tie pasta)
½ cup part-skim ricotta cheese
¼ cup small fresh mint leaves

1. Heat 1 teaspoon oil in a large skillet over medium-high heat. Add lamb; cook 5 minutes, stirring to crumble. Remove lamb from pan with a slotted spoon; sprinkle with ¼ teaspoon salt. Discard drippings from pan. Reduce heat to medium-low. Add 2 teaspoons oil, onion, and carrot; cook 5 minutes or until tender, stirring occasionally. Add rosemary and garlic; cook 1 minute, stirring constantly.

2. Return lamb to pan; add wine. Increase heat to medium-high; cook 3 minutes or until liquid almost evaporates. Add remaining ½ teaspoon salt and pepper. Stir in tomatoes and broth; bring to a simmer. Partially cover and simmer 10 minutes, stirring occasionally.

3. While sauce simmers, cook pasta according to package directions. Drain; return pasta to pan. Stir in 1 cup sauce and remaining 1 teaspoon oil. Spoon 1 cup pasta mixture onto each of 4 plates; top each serving with ¾ cup remaining sauce, 2 tablespoons ricotta, and 1 tablespoon mint. **Yield:** 4 servings.

CALORIES 464; FAT 16.9g (sat 5.9g, mono 7.6g, poly 1.5g); PROTEIN 23.9g; CARB 54.7g; FIBER 4.5g; CHOL 51mg; IRON 4.8mg; SODIUM 629mg; CALC 157mg

a little more...

Serve this with a simple side salad. Combine 1 cup of mixed greens with 1 tablespoon of your favorite vinaigrette for an additional 40 calories.

nutrition note

Pasta

Pasta is a carb-lover's dream. It can also be an easy way to give your diet more whole grains, which provide healthy fats, protein, antioxidants, B vitamins, minerals, and fiber. Look for a whole-grain variety of pasta—the ones that are labeled "whole wheat" and have whole-wheat flour listed first in the ingredient list. If you love the texture and taste of refined pastas and aren't ready to go completely whole-grain, consider doing a mix of whole-grain and refined or using a whole-grain pasta blend.

Fig and Blue Cheese–Stuffed Pork Tenderloin

457 calories

An apple glaze and sweet dried figs complement the savory blue cheese in this simple yet refined dish. Serve with ¾ cup of long-grain and wild rice blend (150 calories) and ¾ cup steamed green beans (33 calories).

- 1 (1-pound) pork tenderloin, trimmed
- ½ cup dried figs, coarsely chopped
- ½ cup (2 ounces) crumbled blue cheese
- ½ teaspoon salt
- ½ teaspoon freshly ground black pepper
- Cooking spray
- 1 tablespoon apple jelly, melted

1. Preheat oven to 450°.

2. Slice pork in half lengthwise, cutting to, but not through, other side. Open halves, laying pork flat. Place pork between 2 sheets of heavy-duty plastic wrap; pound to ½-inch thickness using a meat mallet or small heavy skillet. Sprinkle figs and blue cheese over pork, leaving a ½-inch margin around outside edges. Roll up the pork, jelly-roll fashion, starting with 1 long side. Secure at 2-inch intervals with twine. Sprinkle pork with salt and pepper, and place on a foil-lined jelly-roll pan coated with cooking spray.

3. Bake at 450° for 20 minutes. Brush jelly over pork. Bake an additional 5 minutes or until a thermometer registers 160° (slightly pink). Let stand 10 minutes. Discard twine; cut pork into 12 (1-inch-thick) slices. **Yield:** 4 servings (serving size: 3 slices).

CALORIES 274; FAT 9.2g (sat 4.6g, mono 3g, poly 0.6g); PROTEIN 28.4g; CARB 19.7g; FIBER 2.5g; CHOL 80mg; IRON 1.8mg; SODIUM 581mg; CALC 135mg

a little more...

Serve yourself an extra slice of this delicious stuffed pork. Each slice contains 91 calories.

nutrition note

Figs

Figs are known to have a mild laxative effect. They're also a good source of fiber, manganese, potassium, and vitamin B$_6$.

Pork and Vegetable Stir-Fry with Cashew Rice

Serve a stir-fry loaded with tender pork and crisp veggies. Stir-frying is a great reduced-calorie way to cook, because you use less oil.

¾ cup uncooked long-grain rice

⅓ cup chopped green onions

¼ cup dry-roasted cashews, salted and coarsely chopped

½ teaspoon salt

⅔ cup fat-free, lower-sodium chicken broth

2 tablespoons cornstarch, divided

3 tablespoons lower-sodium soy sauce, divided

2 tablespoons honey

1 (1-pound) pork tenderloin, trimmed and cut into ½-inch cubes

1 tablespoon canola oil, divided

2 cups sliced mushrooms (about 4 ounces)

1 cup chopped onion

1 tablespoon grated peeled fresh ginger

2 garlic cloves, minced

2 cups sugar snap peas (about 6 ounces), trimmed

1 cup chopped red bell pepper (about 1)

1. Cook rice according to package directions, omitting salt and fat. Stir in green onions, cashews, and salt; set aside, and keep warm.

2. Combine broth, 1 tablespoon cornstarch, 2 tablespoons soy sauce, and honey in a small bowl, and set aside.
3. Combine pork, remaining 1 tablespoon cornstarch, and remaining 1 tablespoon soy sauce in a bowl, tossing well to coat. Heat 2 teaspoons oil in a large nonstick skillet over medium-high heat. Add pork; sauté 4 minutes or until browned. Remove from pan.
4. Add remaining 1 teaspoon oil to pan. Add mushrooms and 1 cup onion; sauté 2 minutes. Stir in ginger and garlic; sauté 30 seconds. Add peas and bell pepper to pan; sauté 1 minute. Stir in pork; sauté 1 minute. Add reserved broth mixture to pan. Bring to a boil; cook 1 minute or until thick, stirring constantly. Serve over cashew rice. **Yield:** 4 servings (serving size: 1½ cups pork mixture and ½ cup cashew rice).

CALORIES 460; FAT 11.8g (sat 2.5g, mono 6.2g, poly 2.3g); PROTEIN 31.8g; CARB 55.9g; FIBER 3.6g; CHOL 74mg; IRON 4.6mg; SODIUM 787mg; CALC 73mg

a little more...

Garnish this stir-fry with an extra tablespoon of chopped cashews—they'll add crunch, additional healthy fats, and 50 calories.

nutrition note

Stir-Frying

Stir-frying is one of the fastest and healthiest cooking methods. This method cooks food over high heat, which sears food quickly and preserves the natural juices. It takes only minutes (two to five, usually) and a minimal amount of oil, so vegetables stay bright, crisp, and full of nutrients, and the meat is browned and succulent.

199

Teriyaki Pork and Pineapple

This sweet-salty marinade is excellent for almost any tender cut of meat that's cubed and skewered—chicken breasts or thighs, or beef tenderloin or sirloin. Reducing the marinade concentrates its flavor and helps it stick to the kebabs. Although we usually marinate in zip-top plastic bags, we recommend using a bowl for this recipe so it's easier to scoop out the pork and pineapple with a slotted spoon. Serve over ⅔ cup white and wild rice pilaf—it'll add 174 calories to your meal.

½ cup mirin (sweet rice wine)
½ cup sake (rice wine)
¼ cup lower-sodium soy sauce
1 pound pork tenderloin, trimmed and cut into 24 pieces
24 (1-inch) pieces red onion (about 1 medium)
24 (1-inch) cubes pineapple (about 12 ounces)
Cooking spray

1. Combine first 3 ingredients in a small saucepan; bring to a boil over medium-high heat. Cook until reduced to ⅔ cup (about 10 minutes). Remove from heat; cool completely.
2. Combine cooled marinade and pork in a medium bowl. Cover and marinate in refrigerator 2 hours.
3. Prepare grill to medium-high heat.
4. Remove pork from bowl with a slotted spoon, reserving marinade. Place marinade in a small saucepan; bring to a boil. Reduce heat, and simmer 5 minutes. Cool slightly.
5. Thread 2 pork cubes, 2 red onion pieces, and 2 pineapple cubes alternately onto each of 12 (8-inch) skewers. Lightly coat kebabs with cooking spray. Place kebabs on grill rack coated with cooking spray; grill 3 minutes on each side or until done, basting frequently with marinade.
Yield: 4 servings (serving size: 3 kebabs).

CALORIES 289; FAT 5.4g (sat 1.8g, mono 2g, poly 0.5g); PROTEIN 24.4g; CARB 24.6g; FIBER 1.1g; CHOL 65mg; IRON 1.9mg; SODIUM 580mg; CALC 23mg

a little more...

Serve yourself an extra kebab—it'll add 96 calories to your meal.

nutrition note

Pineapple

Pineapple is an excellent source of vitamin C, which protects you from heart disease, cancer, and cataracts; it also contains manganese, which helps keep your bones strong.

Smoky Slow Cooker Chili

Serve with a piece of corn bread. Although recipes vary, a 1½-ounce piece will add about 130 calories to your meal.

484 calories

Cooking spray
- 1 **pound ground pork**
- 1 **pound boneless pork shoulder, cut into ½-inch pieces**
- 3 **cups chopped onion**
- 1¾ **cups chopped green bell pepper**
- 3 **garlic cloves, minced**
- 3 **tablespoons tomato paste**
- 1 **cup lager-style beer**
- ½ **teaspoon salt, divided**
- 3 **tablespoons chili powder**
- 1 **tablespoon ground cumin**
- 2 **teaspoons dried oregano**
- ¾ **teaspoon black pepper**
- 6 **tomatillos, quartered**
- 2 **bay leaves**
- 2 **(14½-ounce) cans plum tomatoes, undrained and chopped**
- 1 **(15-ounce) can no-salt-added pinto beans, drained**
- 1 **(7¾-ounce) can Mexican hot-style tomato sauce (such as El Paso)**
- 1 **smoked ham hock (about 8 ounces)**
- 1½ **tablespoons sugar**
- ½ **cup finely chopped cilantro**
- ½ **cup finely chopped green onions**
- ½ **cup (2 ounces) crumbled queso fresco**
- 8 **lime wedges**

1. Heat a large nonstick skillet over medium-high heat. Coat pan with cooking spray. Add ground pork to pan; cook 5 minutes or until browned, stirring to slightly crumble. Drain well. Transfer pork to an electric slow cooker.

2. Recoat pan with cooking spray. Add pork shoulder; cook 5 minutes or until lightly browned, turning occasionally. Transfer pork to slow cooker.

3. Recoat pan with cooking spray. Add onion and bell pepper; sauté 8 minutes, stirring frequently. Add garlic; sauté 1 minute. Add tomato paste; cook 1 minute, stirring constantly. Stir in beer; cook 1 minute. Transfer onion mixture to slow cooker. Add ¼ teaspoon salt, chili powder, and next 9 ingredients. Cover and cook on HIGH 5 hours or until meat is tender. Remove bay leaves and ham hock; discard. Stir in remaining ¼ teaspoon salt and sugar. Ladle about 1⅓ cups chili into each of 8 bowls; top each serving with 1 tablespoon cilantro, 1 tablespoon green onions, and 1 tablespoon cheese. Serve each serving with 1 lime wedge. **Yield:** 8 servings.

Note: You can also cook the chili in an electric slow cooker on LOW for 8 hours. For cooking chili on the stovetop, use a total of 12 ounces beer and simmer, covered, for 2½ to 3 hours or until pork shoulder is tender.

CALORIES 354; FAT 14.2g (sat 5.1g, mono 5.9g, poly 1.4g); PROTEIN 28.5g; CARB 26.4g; FIBER 6.8g; CHOL 82mg; IRON 3.8mg; SODIUM 645mg; CALC 108mg

a little more...
Go for a larger side of corn bread. A 2-ounce piece will add 175 calories.

nutrition note

Tomatillos

This firm green fruit resembles small, unripe tomatoes and is often used in Mexican and Latin cuisine. They'll turn yellow as they ripen, but should be used when they're green to take advantage of their wonderful tart flavor. They are a good source of vitamin C.

Risotto with Spring Vegetables and Smoked Ham

¾ cup shelled fava beans (about 1½ pounds unshelled)

2 cups water

2 cups (1-inch) sliced asparagus (about ½ pound)

4 cups fat-free, lower-sodium chicken broth

2 tablespoons extra-virgin olive oil

1 cup finely chopped onion (about 1 small)

½ cup finely chopped smoked ham (about 3 ounces)

1½ cups Arborio rice or other medium-grain rice

1 cup dry white wine

1 cup shelled green peas (about 1 pound unshelled)

¾ cup (3 ounces) grated Parmigiano-Reggiano cheese, divided

¼ cup whipping cream

1 tablespoon butter

½ teaspoon salt

¼ teaspoon freshly ground black pepper

1. Cook beans in boiling water 1 minute; drain. Plunge beans into ice water; drain. Remove tough outer skins from beans; discard skins. Set beans aside.

2. Bring 2 cups water to a boil in a medium saucepan. Add asparagus to pan; cook 4 minutes or until crisp-tender. Remove asparagus from pan with a slotted spoon; rinse under cold water. Set aside.

Add broth to boiling water; reduce heat. Keep warm over low heat. Reserve ¾ cup broth mixture; keep warm.

3. Heat olive oil in a large saucepan over medium heat. Add onion and ham to pan; cook 10 minutes or until onion is tender, stirring occasionally. Add rice; cook 2 minutes, stirring frequently. Increase heat to medium-high. Stir in wine, and cook 2 minutes or until liquid is nearly absorbed, stirring constantly. Add remaining broth mixture, ½ cup at a time, stirring constantly until each portion of broth is absorbed before adding the next (about 25 minutes total).

4. Stir in peas, reserved beans, and reserved asparagus. Add reserved ¾ cup broth mixture, stirring until liquid is absorbed (about 4 minutes). Remove from heat; stir in ½ cup cheese, cream, butter, salt, and pepper. Place about 1 cup risotto into each of 6 shallow bowls; sprinkle each serving with 2 teaspoons remaining cheese. **Yield:** 6 servings.

CALORIES 439; FAT 14.4g (sat 6.1g, mono 6g, poly 1.1g); PROTEIN 19.7g; CARB 59.4g; FIBER 9.8g; CHOL 31mg; IRON 3.3mg; SODIUM 758mg; CALC 173mg

a little more...

To contrast the rich flavor and creamy texture of the risotto, pair this meal with 1 cup of fresh sliced strawberries. It'll add 60 calories to your meal.

nutrition note

Fava Beans

Fava beans are a nutrient-rich food. They're high in protein, iron, and fiber, and are a good source of potassium and vitamins C and A.

Pear and Prosciutto Pizza

Pit peppery arugula against a base of creamy, sweet caramelized onions. Also appearing: prudent amounts of salty prosciutto, cheese, and walnuts.

446 calories

2   teaspoons olive oil
2   cups vertically sliced Oso Sweet or other sweet onion
1   (12-ounce) prebaked pizza crust (such as Mama Mary's)
½   cup (2 ounces) shredded provolone cheese
1   medium pear, thinly sliced
2   ounces prosciutto, cut into thin strips
    Dash of freshly ground black pepper
2   tablespoons chopped walnuts, toasted
1½ cups baby arugula leaves
1   teaspoon sherry vinegar

1. Preheat oven to 450°.
2. Heat oil in a large nonstick skillet over medium-high heat. Add onion to pan; cover and cook 3 minutes. Uncover and cook 10 minutes or until golden brown, stirring frequently.
3. Place pizza crust on a baking sheet. Top evenly with onion mixture; sprinkle with cheese. Top evenly with pear and prosciutto. Sprinkle with pepper. Bake at 450° for 12 minutes or until cheese melts. Sprinkle with nuts. Place arugula in a medium bowl. Drizzle vinegar over greens; toss gently to coat. Top pizza evenly with arugula mixture. Cut pizza into 8 wedges. **Yield:** 4 servings (serving size: 2 wedges).

CALORIES 446; FAT 18.8g (sat 4.9g, mono 5.1g, poly 7.3g); PROTEIN 16.6g; CARB 55.5g; FIBER 3.8g; CHOL 17mg; IRON 3.6mg; SODIUM 664mg; CALC 221mg

a little more...

Serve yourself an extra slice—it'll add 223 calories to your meal.

nutrition note

Healthy Pizza

Pizza can be healthy (as the recipe at left shows). One way to ensure it stays that way is bulking it up with fresh vegetables (like spinach and mushrooms)—it helps you feel full and more satisfied with less food.

Chicken Breasts with Mushroom Sauce

452 calories

Butter and whipping cream add a wonderful lushness to this savory pan gravy, which features fresh morel and button mushrooms.

6 (6-ounce) skinless, boneless chicken breast halves
3 tablespoons butter, divided
½ teaspoon salt
¼ teaspoon freshly ground black pepper
4 ounces morel mushrooms
4 ounces button mushrooms, thinly sliced
2 cups fat-free, lower-sodium chicken broth
¼ cup whipping cream
4½ cups hot cooked egg noodles
  Flat-leaf parsley sprigs (optional)

1. Place each chicken breast half between 2 sheets of heavy-duty plastic wrap; flatten to ¼-inch thickness using a meat mallet or small heavy skillet. Heat 2 teaspoons butter in a large nonstick skillet over medium heat. Sprinkle chicken evenly with salt and pepper. Add 2 breast halves to pan, and cook 3 minutes on each side or until done. Repeat procedure twice with 4 teaspoons butter and remaining chicken. Keep warm.

2. Melt remaining 1 tablespoon butter in pan over medium-high heat. Add mushrooms to pan; sauté 5 minutes or until moisture evaporates, stirring frequently. Remove mushroom mixture from pan. Add broth to pan; bring to a boil, scraping pan to loosen browned bits. Cook until reduced to 1 cup (about 5 minutes). Return mushroom mixture to pan. Stir in cream; cook 2 minutes or until slightly thick, stirring occasionally.

3. Place ¾ cup egg noodles on each of 6 plates. Cut each chicken breast half into 1-inch-thick strips. Top each serving with 1 chicken breast half and about ⅓ cup mushroom mixture. Garnish each serving with parsley sprigs, if desired. **Yield:** 6 servings.

CALORIES 452; FAT 14.2g (sat 7g, mono 3.8g, poly 1.6g); PROTEIN 47g; CARB 32.2g; FIBER 2.2g; CHOL 162mg; IRON 3.4mg; SODIUM 489mg; CALC 49mg

a little more...

Pair this meal with ¾ cup of fresh green peas for an additional 88 calories.

nutrition note

Butter vs. Margarine

Most margarines are made using a method called hydrogenation, which creates unhealthy trans fats, and, in general, the more solid the margarine, the more trans fats it contains. Trans fats have been linked to heart and arterial disease and should be avoided. While butter is made from animal fats and contains more saturated fat than margarine, it doesn't contain trans fats and can add richness and enhance the flavor of a dish. The best advice: Use butter in moderation.

Almond-Stuffed Chicken

The nutty, cheesy filling spices up chicken breasts and is a snap to make. Toast the almonds in a skillet before you cook the chicken and you'll have just one pan to clean. Serve with ⅔ cup each of couscous and haricots verts. These two sides add 140 calories for a complete meal.

428 calories

⅓ cup light garlic-and-herbs spreadable cheese
¼ cup slivered almonds, toasted, coarsely chopped, and divided
3 tablespoons chopped fresh parsley, divided
4 (6-ounce) skinless, boneless chicken breast halves
½ teaspoon salt
¼ teaspoon freshly ground black pepper
1½ teaspoons butter

1. Combine spreadable cheese, 3 tablespoons almonds, and 2 tablespoons parsley in a small bowl. Set aside.
2. Cut a horizontal slit through thickest portion of each breast half to form a pocket. Stuff 1½ tablespoons almond mixture into each pocket; secure each pocket with a wooden pick. Sprinkle chicken with salt and pepper.
3. Heat butter in a large nonstick skillet over medium heat. Add chicken to pan; cook 6 minutes on each side or until done. Remove from pan; cover and let stand 2 minutes. Top chicken evenly with remaining 1 tablespoon almonds and remaining 1 tablespoon parsley.
Yield: 4 servings (serving size: 1 stuffed chicken breast half, about 1 teaspoon almonds, and about 1 teaspoon parsley).

CALORIES 288; FAT 12.7g (sat 4.3g, mono 4.5g, poly 1.8g); PROTEIN 37.5g; CARB 3.9g; FIBER 0.9g; CHOL 111mg; IRON 1.7mg; SODIUM 496mg; CALC 109mg

a little more...

For an extra nutty crunch, toast 1 tablespoon of almonds to go on top of your couscous. It'll add 39 calories.

nutrition note

The Power of Nuts

Nuts are great for you. They contain heart-healthy mono- and polyunsaturated fats that can help lower your cholesterol, as well as protein, vitamin E, folate, and magnesium, plus a small amount of fiber and iron. This mix of nutrients helps keep you full longer, but portion control is key since the calories in nuts can add up quickly.

211

Cilantro-Lime Chicken with Avocado Salsa

Serve with Saffron Rice—a ½-cup serving will add 196 calories to your meal.

2 tablespoons minced fresh cilantro
2½ tablespoons fresh lime juice
1½ tablespoons olive oil
4 (6-ounce) skinless, boneless chicken breast halves
¼ teaspoon salt
Cooking spray
1 cup chopped plum tomato (about 2)
2 tablespoons finely chopped onion
2 teaspoons fresh lime juice
¼ teaspoon salt
⅛ teaspoon freshly ground black pepper
1 avocado, peeled and finely chopped

1. Combine first 4 ingredients in a large bowl; toss and let stand 3 minutes. Remove chicken from marinade; discard marinade. Sprinkle chicken evenly with ¼ teaspoon salt. Heat a grill pan over medium-high heat. Coat pan with cooking spray. Add chicken to pan; cook 6 minutes on each side or until done.
2. Combine tomato and next 4 ingredients in a medium bowl. Add avocado; stir gently to combine. Serve salsa over chicken. **Yield:** 4 servings (serving size: 1 chicken breast half and about ¼ cup salsa).

CALORIES 289; FAT 13.2g (sat 2.4g, mono 7.5g, poly 1.9g); PROTEIN 35.6g; CARB 6.6g; FIBER 3.6g; CHOL 94mg; IRON 1.6mg; SODIUM 383mg; CALC 29mg

Saffron Rice

Cooking spray
1 cup diced onion
2 garlic cloves, minced
1 cup uncooked basmati rice
2 cups fat-free, lower-sodium chicken broth
¼ teaspoon saffron threads, crushed
Bay leaf

1. Heat a medium saucepan over medium heat. Coat pan with cooking spray. Add onion and garlic to pan; cook 5 minutes or until golden brown, stirring frequently. Add rice and next 3 ingredients; bring to a boil. Cover, reduce heat, and simmer 20 minutes. Discard bay leaf. **Yield:** 4 servings (serving size: ¾ cup).

CALORIES 196; FAT 0.1g (sat 0g, mono 0g, poly 0g); PROTEIN 5g; CARB 43.8g; FIBER 1.7g; CHOL 0mg; IRON 0.5mg; SODIUM 287mg; CALC 32mg

a little more...

Fresh fruit would be a nice contrast to the rich, creamy avocado salsa. A 1-cup serving of fresh cantaloupe would add 54 calories to your meal.

nutrition note

Marinating

Marinating is a versatile and indispensable technique. It boosts the flavor of lean cuts of meat and also works wonders with fruits and vegetables, bringing variety and new life to foods that may make a common appearance in your kitchen. The marinade in this recipe relies on fresh herbs, lemon juice, and olive oil—healthy ingredients that add loads of flavor.

Bacon, Ranch, and Chicken Mac and Cheese

A tablespoon of flour stabilizes the milk so that you can bring the sauce to a boil. The combination of onion and garlic powders plus fresh dill creates a flavor similar to ranch dressing.

8 ounces uncooked elbow macaroni
1 slice applewood-smoked bacon
8 ounces skinless, boneless chicken breast, cut into ½-inch pieces
1 tablespoon butter
1 tablespoon all-purpose flour
1½ cups fat-free milk
⅓ cup condensed 45% reduced-sodium 98% fat-free cream of mushroom soup, undiluted
¾ cup (3 ounces) shredded 6-cheese Italian blend (such as Sargento)
½ teaspoon onion powder
½ teaspoon garlic powder
½ teaspoon chopped fresh dill
½ teaspoon salt
Cooking spray
½ cup (2 ounces) shredded colby-Jack cheese

1. Cook pasta according to package directions, omitting salt and fat; drain.
2. Cook bacon in a large nonstick skillet over medium heat until crisp. Remove bacon from pan, reserving drippings in pan. Finely chop bacon; set aside. Increase heat to medium-high. Add chicken to drippings in pan; sauté 6 minutes or until done.
3. Melt butter in a large saucepan over medium heat; sprinkle flour evenly into pan. Cook 2 minutes, stirring constantly with a whisk. Combine milk and soup, stirring with a whisk; gradually add milk mixture to saucepan, stirring with a whisk. Bring to a boil; cook 2 minutes or until thick. Remove from heat; let stand 4 minutes or until sauce cools to 155°. Add Italian cheese blend and next 4 ingredients, stirring until cheese melts. Stir in pasta and chicken.
4. Preheat broiler.
5. Spoon mixture into an 8-inch square baking dish coated with cooking spray. Sprinkle evenly with reserved bacon and colby-Jack cheese. Broil 3 minutes or until cheese melts. **Yield:** 4 servings (serving size: about 2 cups).

CALORIES 497; FAT 17g (sat 9.2g, mono 4.7g, poly 1.4g); PROTEIN 33.3g; CARB 51.7g; FIBER 2g; CHOL 74mg; IRON 2.4mg; SODIUM 767mg; CALC 368mg

a little more...

Serve with ¾ cup steamed green beans. It'll add 33 calories to your meal.

nutrition note

Cheese in Mac and Cheese

One of the nutritional perks of this cheesy recipe is that one serving provides about one-fourth of your daily calcium needs. If you're thinking about making a cheese substitution in the recipe, you need to pick the proper cheese for the best texture. Avoid hard, aged cheeses; they don't melt easily or smoothly.

Spicy Honey-Brushed Chicken Thighs

446 calories

One of the most popular *Cooking Light* chicken recipes, these sweet and spicy grilled chicken thighs are flavored with chili powder, cumin, garlic, and cider vinegar. Serve with ¾ cup roasted potato wedges (75 calories) and 1 cup of a simple side salad of mixed greens, tomatoes, and matchstick-cut carrots with 1 tablespoon of your favorite vinaigrette (50 calories).

2 teaspoons garlic powder
2 teaspoons chili powder
1 teaspoon salt
1 teaspoon ground cumin
1 teaspoon paprika
½ teaspoon ground red pepper
8 skinless, boneless chicken thighs
Cooking spray
6 tablespoons honey
2 teaspoons cider vinegar

1. Preheat broiler.
2. Combine first 6 ingredients in a large bowl. Add chicken to bowl; toss to coat. Place chicken on a broiler pan coated with cooking spray. Broil chicken 5 minutes on each side.

3. Combine honey and vinegar in a small bowl, stirring well. Remove chicken from oven; brush ¼ cup honey mixture on chicken. Broil 1 minute. Remove chicken from oven and turn pieces over. Brush chicken with remaining honey mixture. Broil 1 minute or until chicken is done.
Yield: 4 servings (serving size: 2 chicken thighs).

CALORIES 321; FAT 11g (sat 3g, mono 4.1g, poly 2.5g); PROTEIN 28g; CARB 27.9g; FIBER 0.6g; CHOL 99mg; IRON 2.1mg; SODIUM 676mg; CALC 21mg

a little more...

A nice contrast to the spicy chicken would be cool fresh watermelon. A cup will add 46 calories.

nutrition note

Chicken Thighs

While chicken thighs contain slightly higher levels of calories and fat than chicken breasts, they have a wonderfully rich flavor. By simply removing the skin, you'll consume 15 percent fewer calories and 28 percent less saturated fat.

Chicken Carne Asada Tacos with Pickled Onions

455 calories

Pair with a serving of Spicy Black Beans for an additional 42 calories.

½ cup fresh orange juice
⅓ cup fresh lime juice (about 2 limes)
1 teaspoon sugar
1 teaspoon cumin seeds
1 medium red onion, thinly vertically sliced
1½ pounds skinless, boneless chicken thighs, trimmed and cut into thin strips
1 teaspoon dried oregano
1 teaspoon ground cumin
¾ teaspoon salt
¾ teaspoon freshly ground black pepper
Cooking spray
8 (6-inch) corn tortillas
1 cup diced peeled avocado
½ cup (2 ounces) crumbled Cotija cheese

1. Combine first 4 ingredients in a medium bowl, stirring until sugar dissolves. Place onion in a small saucepan; cover with water. Bring to a boil; drain and plunge onion in ice water. Drain onion; add to juice mixture. Chill until ready to serve.
2. Heat a large cast-iron skillet over high heat. Sprinkle chicken with oregano, cumin, salt, and pepper; toss to coat. Coat pan with cooking spray. Add chicken to pan; cook 4 minutes or until browned and done, stirring occasionally.
3. Heat tortillas according to package directions. Divide chicken evenly among tortillas. Drain onion; divide evenly among tortillas. Top each tortilla with 2 tablespoons avocado and 1 tablespoon cheese; fold over. **Yield:** 4 servings (serving size: 2 tacos).

CALORIES 413; FAT 17.1g (sat 5.2g, mono 7.1g, poly 2.7g); PROTEIN 33.4g; CARB 33.6g; FIBER 4.9g; CHOL 123mg; IRON 3.2mg; SODIUM 825mg; CALC 237mg

Spicy Black Beans

1 (7-ounce) can chipotle chiles in adobo sauce
¼ cup fat-free, lower-sodium chicken broth
1 (15-ounce) can black beans, rinsed and drained
1 tablespoon chopped fresh cilantro

1. Remove 1 teaspoon adobo sauce from can of chipotle chiles in adobo sauce; reserve remaining chiles and sauce for another use. Combine 1 teaspoon adobo sauce, broth, and beans in a saucepan; bring to a boil. Mash bean mixture. Sprinkle with cilantro. **Yield:** 4 servings.

CALORIES 42; FAT 0.8g (sat 0g, mono 0.2g, poly 0g); PROTEIN 2.9g; CARB 11g; FIBER 3.7g; CHOL 0mg; IRON 0.8mg; SODIUM 493mg; CALC 23mg

a little more...

Serve yourself an extra taco (207 calories) or, for some crunch, prepare Easy Guacamole (page 188), and pair a serving (94 calories) with 15 light baked tortilla chips (155 calories).

back on track

Serve Good-for-You Foods Family-Style

Not all portion-control strategies are about eating less. You can have as much as you want of some foods. Place the foods you want your family to eat more of—salads and vegetable sides—within easy reach on the dining table.

Tex-Mex Calzones

416 calories

Spice up sandwich night with this Tex-Mex–inspired favorite packed with ground turkey, fresh veggies, and spicy salsa.

8 ounces ground turkey breast
½ cup chopped onion
½ cup chopped green bell pepper
½ cup chopped red bell pepper
¾ teaspoon ground cumin
½ teaspoon chili powder
2 garlic cloves, minced
½ cup fat-free fire-roasted salsa verde
1 (11-ounce) can refrigerated thin-crust pizza dough
¾ cup (3 ounces) preshredded 4-cheese Mexican blend cheese
Cooking spray
¼ cup fat-free sour cream

1. Preheat oven to 425°.
2. Heat a large nonstick skillet over medium-high heat. Add ground turkey to pan; cook 3 minutes, stirring to crumble. Add onion and next 5 ingredients to pan; cook 4 minutes or until vegetables are crisp-tender, stirring mixture occasionally. Remove turkey mixture from heat; stir in salsa.
3. Unroll dough; divide into 4 equal portions. Roll each portion into a 6 x 4–inch rectangle. Working with 1 rectangle at a time, spoon about ½ cup turkey mixture on 1 side of dough. Top with 3 tablespoons cheese; fold dough over turkey mixture, and press edges together with a fork to seal. Place on a baking sheet coated with cooking spray. Repeat procedure with remaining dough and turkey mixture. Bake at 425° for 12 minutes or until browned. Serve with sour cream. **Yield:** 4 servings (serving size: 1 calzone and 1 tablespoon sour cream).

CALORIES 416; FAT 14.1g (sat 6.1g, mono 4.9g, poly 1.6g); PROTEIN 25.7g; CARB 46.2g; FIBER 2.5g; CHOL 44mg; IRON 2.5mg; SODIUM 771mg; CALC 195mg

a little more...

Pair these calzones with a serving of Black Bean Salad for an additional 85 calories.

Black Bean Salad

1 (15-ounce) can black beans, rinsed and drained
1 cup quartered cherry tomatoes
½ cup chopped red onion
¼ cup chopped celery
2 tablespoons fresh lime juice
2 tablespoons chopped fresh cilantro
1 tablespoon olive oil

1. Combine all ingredients in a medium bowl; toss well to coat. **Yield:** 4 servings.

CALORIES 85; FAT 4g (sat 0.5g, mono 2.5g, poly 0.4g); PROTEIN 3.3g; CARB 14.8g; FIBER 4.7g; CHOL 0mg; IRON 1mg; SODIUM 210mg; CALC 34mg

nutrition note

Ground Turkey

Not all ground turkey is created equal. Regular ground turkey (labeled 93 percent lean) is a combination of white and dark meat and is fairly high in calories and fat, but it's still leaner than ground round (usually 85 percent lean). Frozen ground turkey, which is all dark meat and can contain skin, can be just as high in fat as ground beef (80 percent lean or less). Ground turkey breast is the lowest in fat, but it can dry out. It's best used in saucy and soupy applications to keep it from becoming dry.

Tomato-Ricotta Spaghetti

437 calories

Roasting tomatoes intensifies their sweetness. Serve a 1½-ounce piece of French bread with this pasta. It'll provide 123 calories.

- 2 **pints cherry tomatoes, halved (about 4 cups)**
- 5 **teaspoons extra-virgin olive oil, divided**
- ½ **teaspoon salt, divided**
- 8 **ounces uncooked spaghetti**
- ½ **cup (2 ounces) ricotta salata cheese, crumbled**
- ⅓ **cup chopped fresh basil**
- ¼ **teaspoon freshly ground black pepper**

1. Preheat oven to 400°.

2. Place tomatoes on a foil-lined baking sheet. Drizzle with 1 teaspoon oil; sprinkle with ⅛ teaspoon salt. Bake at 400° for 20 minutes or until tomatoes collapse.

3. Cook pasta according to package directions, omitting salt and fat. Drain pasta in a colander over a bowl, reserving ⅓ cup cooking liquid. Return pasta and reserved liquid to pan; stir in tomatoes, remaining 4 teaspoons oil, remaining ⅜ teaspoon salt, cheese, basil, and pepper. Toss well. Serve immediately. **Yield:** 4 servings (serving size: 1¼ cups).

CALORIES 314; FAT 8.4g (sat 1.8g, mono 4.7g, poly 1.4g); PROTEIN 10.5g; CARB 50.3g; FIBER 3.6g; CHOL 5mg; IRON 2.7mg; SODIUM 331mg; CALC 66mg

a little more...

Serve yourself a larger 1½-cup portion, which will provide 377 calories.

nutrition note

Ricotta Salata

In addition to the fresh soft form of ricotta cheese (often used in lasagna), another variety is ricotta salata. It's a dry salted ricotta cheese that has been pressed. This sheep's milk cheese is pure white, firm, and dense, and has a sharp, tangy flavor. (In Italian, ricotta simply means "recooked," referring to the cheese-making process rather than the cheese. Salata means "salted.") While this variety is slightly higher in calories and sodium than regular ricotta, the flavor and texture are irreplaceable.

Goat Cheese and Roasted Corn Quesadillas

473 calories

Browning the corn caramelizes its sugars and deepens the taste of this dish. If you have fresh cilantro on hand, chop 2 tablespoons and stir it into the salsa. Serve with ¾ cup yellow rice (145 calories) and ¾ cup black beans (105 calories) for a tasty vegetarian meal.

- 1 **cup fresh corn kernels (about 1 large ear)**
- ⅔ **cup (5 ounces) goat cheese, softened**
- 8 **(6-inch) corn tortillas**
- ¼ **cup chopped green onions (about 1 green onion)**
- 10 **tablespoons bottled salsa verde, divided**
- **Cooking spray**

1. Heat a large nonstick skillet over medium-high heat. Add corn; sauté 2 minutes or until browned. Place corn in a small bowl. Add goat cheese to corn; stir until well blended. Divide corn mixture evenly among 4 tortillas; spread to within ¼ inch of sides. Sprinkle each tortilla with 1 tablespoon green onions. Drizzle each with 1½ teaspoons salsa; top with remaining 4 tortillas.

2. Heat pan over medium-high heat. Coat pan with cooking spray. Place 2 quesadillas in pan; cook 1½ minutes on each side or until golden. Remove from pan; keep warm. Wipe pan clean with paper towels; recoat with cooking spray. Repeat procedure with remaining quesadillas. Cut each quesadilla into 4 wedges. Serve with remaining 8 tablespoons salsa. **Yield:** 4 servings (serving size: 4 wedges and 2 tablespoons salsa).

CALORIES 223; FAT 8.9g (sat 5.2g, mono 1.8g, poly 0.9g); PROTEIN 9.9g; CARB 28.6g; FIBER 3.2g; CHOL 16mg; IRON 1mg; SODIUM 266mg; CALC 75mg

a little more…

Add ⅓ cup of chopped cooked chicken breast to these quesadillas for some extra protein and bulk. This will add 77 calories and 14.5 grams of protein.

nutrition note

Corn

Corn is delicious and healthful. It's naturally low in saturated fat and sodium, contains B vitamins, folate, and dietary fiber, and is a good source of vitamin C.

dinner

225

Black Bean Burgers with Mango Salsa

Pair this meatless burger with veggie chips, which will add 150 calories per 1-ounce serving (about 14 chips).

2 (15-ounce) cans black beans, rinsed and drained
¾ cup finely chopped fresh cilantro, divided
¾ cup (3 ounces) shredded Monterey Jack cheese
¼ cup panko (Japanese breadcrumbs)
2 teaspoons ground cumin
1 teaspoon dried oregano
½ teaspoon sea salt
½ medium jalapeño pepper, finely chopped
2 large egg whites
Cooking spray
1¼ cups chopped peeled mango (about 1 medium)
3 tablespoons chopped shallots
1½ tablespoons fresh lime juice
1 avocado, peeled and chopped
1 garlic clove, minced
6 (2-ounce) whole-wheat hamburger buns, lightly toasted
6 green leaf lettuce leaves

1. Preheat oven to 350°.
2. Place black beans in a medium bowl; mash with a fork. Stir in ½ cup finely chopped cilantro and next 7 ingredients. Shape bean mixture into 6 (½-inch-thick) patties. Arrange patties on a baking sheet coated with cooking spray. Bake at 350° for 20 minutes, carefully turning once.
3. Combine remaining ¼ cup cilantro, mango, and next 4 ingredients in a medium bowl. Place 1 patty on bottom half of each hamburger bun; top each with 1 lettuce leaf, ⅓ cup salsa, and top half of bun. **Yield:** 6 servings (serving size: 1 burger).

CALORIES 320; FAT 11.9g (sat 3.9g, mono 5g, poly 1.7g); PROTEIN 13.4g; CARB 46.2g; FIBER 10.1g; CHOL 13mg; IRON 3.3mg; SODIUM 777mg; CALC 201mg

a little more...

Add a slice of Monterey Jack cheese to amp up this burger. A 1-ounce slice will add 110 calories and 6 grams of protein.

nutrition note

Mango

In addition to great tropical flavor, mangoes provide a variety of nutrients. They're an excellent source of vitamins A and C, a good source of fiber, and contain over 20 different additional vitamins and minerals.

snacks

- Healthy Ideas for Snacks
- Eating Out Tips
- Recipes

snacks

The moment a favorite snack or dessert hits your taste buds, your brain sends out soothing *ahh* chemicals. For many of us, guilt soon follows. Yet it's easy to snack smart and eat dessert without guilt—and instead enjoy both with pleasure. The right snacks supply important nutrients, keep you satisfied between meals, boost energy, and lift your mood. And because food is meant to be pleasurable and part of the pleasure is treating yourself, desserts shouldn't be forbidden. A healthy approach to eating includes permission to satisfy that part of the soul that craves desserts—in proper portions.

Healthy Ideas for Snacking

• **Limit your choices.** The more options you have, the more you want to try. In one study, researchers gave two groups jellybeans to snack on while they watched a movie. One group got six colors, neatly divided into compartments; jellybeans for the other group were jumbled together. Those given a mix ate nearly two times more.

• **Eat a combination of complex carbohydrates and lean protein** with each snack. This mix helps keep your blood sugar stable, which can help you achieve and maintain a healthy weight. For example, sprinkle low-fat yogurt with high-fiber cereal, spread peanut butter on a slice of whole-wheat toast and top with half of a banana, or dress a small baked potato with low-fat cheese and salsa.

• **Plan ahead.** If you work eight or more hours a day, it can be difficult to eat healthfully unless you plan ahead. Research shows that eating every four hours helps to keep your metabolism charged and your energy level high. Before you dig into your drawer for spare change and head to the vending machine, plan ahead and stash low-calorie, nutritious snacks in a cabinet, drawer, or your briefcase.

• **Remember whole fruit.** Fruit is a no-brainer when it comes to snacks because it's one of the easiest grab-and-go foods available. Pick up a week's supply at the grocery store and take some with you to work or keep it out on the counter at home so it'll be right there for you to pick up. But it's easy to get stuck in a rut of buying the same fruits again and again. Avoid this habit by shopping for what's in season. You'll enjoy ephemeral flavors plus nutritional variety as your choices change naturally through the year.

Eating Out Tips

If you aren't able to bring your own snacks, here are some ideas when swinging through a drive-thru, stopping at a convenience store, or standing in front of the vending machine:

• *A 1.5-ounce package of tropical trail mix* = 180 calories
• *Junior-sized Chocolate Frosty from Wendy's* = 150 calories
• *Vanilla Ice Cream Cone (reduced-fat) at McDonald's* = 150 calories

good choice:
1 apple + 1 tablespoon peanut butter = 189 calories and 5.7 grams of filling fiber

not-so-good choices:
1 slice of cake = 600 calories
1 medium serving of fries = 370 calories
1 (1.5-ounce) serving of potato chips = 225 calories

Hot Artichoke-Cheese Dip

This warm dip is just the thing when you hanker for a creamy, cheesy snack. And because you are likely to have the ingredients on hand in the fridge and freezer, it's also great for impromptu entertaining.

126 calories

2 garlic cloves
1 green onion, cut into pieces
⅓ cup (1½ ounces) grated Parmigiano-Reggiano cheese, divided
⅓ cup reduced-fat mayonnaise
¼ cup (2 ounces) ⅓-less-fat cream cheese
1 tablespoon fresh lemon juice
¼ teaspoon crushed red pepper
12 ounces frozen artichoke hearts, thawed and drained
   Cooking spray
24 (½-ounce) slices baguette, toasted

1. Preheat oven to 400°.
2. Place garlic and onion in a food processor; process until finely chopped.

Add ¼ cup Parmigiano-Reggiano cheese and next 4 ingredients; process until almost smooth. Add artichoke hearts; pulse until artichoke hearts are coarsely chopped. Spoon mixture into a 3-cup gratin dish coated with cooking spray; sprinkle evenly with remaining Parmigiano-Reggiano cheese. Bake at 400° for 15 minutes or until thoroughly heated and bubbly. Serve hot with baguette slices. **Yield:** 12 servings (serving size: 2½ tablespoons dip and 2 baguette slices).

CALORIES 126; FAT 3.4g (sat 1.3g, mono 0.6g, poly 0.5g); PROTEIN 5.1g; CARB 20.8g; FIBER 2.3g; CHOL 7mg; IRON 1.1mg; SODIUM 334mg; CALC 59mg

back on track

Avoid a See-Food Diet

Office workers who kept candy in clear dishes on their desks dipped in for a sample 71 percent more often than those who kept their candy out of sight. If you keep candy in your work space, put it in a drawer or container where it's not in your view all day.

Party Bean Dip with Baked Tortilla Chips

135 calories

Making your own tortilla chips helps manage fat levels, allowing you to use regular cheese in the recipe. Organic refried beans may have at least half the sodium of conventional ones and can have a drier texture. Adding a little lime juice makes the beans smoother and enhances the flavor. Using organic salsa also helps keep sodium in check.

6 (8-inch) fat-free flour tortillas
Cooking spray
½ teaspoon paprika
2 teaspoons fresh lime juice
½ teaspoon ground cumin
1 (16-ounce) can organic refried beans (such as Amy's or Eden Organic)
1 cup organic bottled salsa (such as Muir Glen)
⅔ cup frozen whole-kernel corn, thawed
¼ cup chopped green onions
2 tablespoons chopped black olives
¾ cup (3 ounces) preshredded 4-cheese Mexican blend cheese
¾ cup light sour cream
2 tablespoons chopped fresh cilantro

1. Preheat oven to 350°.
2. Cut each tortilla into 8 wedges, and arrange wedges in single layers on 2 baking sheets. Lightly spray wedges with cooking spray; sprinkle with paprika. Bake at 350° for 15 minutes or until lightly browned and crisp. Cool.
3. Combine juice, cumin, and beans in a medium bowl, stirring until well combined. Spread mixture evenly into an 11 x 7–inch baking dish coated with cooking spray. Spread salsa evenly over beans. Combine corn, onions, and olives; spoon corn mixture evenly over salsa. Sprinkle cheese over corn mixture. Bake at 350° for 20 minutes or until bubbly. Let stand 10 minutes. Top with sour cream; sprinkle with cilantro. Serve with tortilla chips. **Yield:** 12 servings (serving size: ½ cup dip and 4 tortilla wedges).

CALORIES 135; FAT 3.8g (sat 2.3g, mono 0.1g, poly 0.1g); PROTEIN 6.1g; CARB 20.7g; FIBER 4g; CHOL 11mg; IRON 1.1mg; SODIUM 392mg; CALC 123mg

nutrition note

Refried Beans

Traditionally, refried beans are made using lard, which is high in saturated fat, but you can find many canned varieties that are made using vegetable oil. With a lower amount of saturated fat, these varieties are healthier options. Another healthy choice is a fat-free variety, which is made without lard or oil—just beans, seasonings, and spices. Read the ingredient label to be sure what you're buying.

Spicy Black Bean Hummus

This delicious hummus comes together quickly.

148 calories

1 garlic clove, peeled
2 tablespoons fresh lemon juice
1 tablespoon tahini (roasted sesame seed paste)
1 teaspoon ground cumin
¼ teaspoon salt
1 (15-ounce) can black beans, rinsed and drained
1 small jalapeño pepper, chopped (about 2 tablespoons)
Dash of crushed red pepper
2 teaspoons extra-virgin olive oil
Dash of ground red pepper
1 (6-ounce) bag pita chips (such as Stacy's Simply Naked)

1. Place garlic in a food processor; process until finely chopped. Add lemon juice and next 6 ingredients; process until smooth.

2. Spoon bean mixture into a medium bowl, and drizzle with oil. Sprinkle with ground red pepper. Serve with pita chips. **Yield:** 8 servings (serving size: about 2½ tablespoons hummus and 4 chips).

CALORIES 148; FAT 6.2g (sat 0.7g, mono 1.2g, poly 0.6g); PROTEIN 4.5g; CARB 20.6g; FIBER 3.5g; CHOL 0mg; IRON 1.7mg; SODIUM 381mg; CALC 16mg

nutrition note

Black Beans

This rich-tasting bean has a velvety texture and also offers a variety of nutritional benefits. Like other beans, it's high in fiber and protein—a ½ cup of cooked beans provides 7.5 grams of fiber and 7.6 grams of protein. They're also rich in folate and magnesium.

Lima Bean Dip

Fava beans are traditional in this hummus-like dip. Use them, if you can find them, in place of the lima beans. Serve with raw vegetables for dipping. A 1-cup serving of a mixture of fresh carrots, bell pepper strips, celery, and cucumber will add 27 calories.

122 calories

1 **pound frozen baby lima beans**
3 **tablespoons sesame seeds, toasted**
¼ **cup fresh lemon juice**
1 **tablespoon extra-virgin olive oil**
¾ **teaspoon kosher salt**
1 **garlic clove**

1. Cook beans in boiling water 10 minutes or until very tender. Drain, reserving ½ cup cooking liquid.

2. Place sesame seeds in a blender; process until finely ground. Add juice and next 3 ingredients; process until blended. Add beans and ½ cup reserved liquid; process until almost smooth, scraping sides of blender occasionally. **Yield:** 8 servings (serving size: about ¼ cup).

CALORIES 95; FAT 3.4g (sat 0.3g, mono 1.4g, poly 0.2g); PROTEIN 4.7g; CARB 13g; FIBER 3.6g; CHOL 0mg; IRON 1.4mg; SODIUM 195mg; CALC 21mg

nutrition note

Lima Beans

Lima beans are loaded with nutrients. They're a good source of fiber and protein—a ½ cup of cooked lima beans contains 7 grams of fiber and 7.3 grams of protein. They're also a good source of folate, potassium, and iron.

White Bean Dip with Rosemary and Sage

128 calories

Prepare the dip up to a day in advance to give the flavors a chance to meld. In addition to pita wedges, you can serve mixed fresh vegetables for dipping.

2 tablespoons fresh lemon juice
1 tablespoon extra-virgin olive oil
2 teaspoons minced fresh rosemary
2 teaspoons minced fresh sage
¼ teaspoon freshly ground black pepper
2 garlic cloves, chopped
1 (19-ounce) can cannellini beans or other white beans, rinsed and drained
4 (6-inch) pitas, each cut into 6 wedges
Fresh sage sprig (optional)

1. Place first 7 ingredients in a food processor; process until smooth. Serve with pita wedges. Garnish with sage sprig, if desired. **Yield:** 8 servings (serving size: about 3 tablespoons dip and 3 pita wedges).

CALORIES 128; FAT 1.9g (sat 0.3g, mono 1.3g, poly 0.3g); PROTEIN 5.1g; CARB 22.6g; FIBER 2.1g; CHOL 0mg; IRON 1.9mg; SODIUM 161mg; CALC 35mg

nutrition note

Include Protein

Eating a snack with protein (like the beans in this recipe) rather than just carbs can help curb hunger, keeping daily calories in check.

Avocado-Mango Salsa with Roasted Corn Chips

Avocado provides more than half of the 158 milligrams of potassium in each serving of this snack, which is also a good source of fiber and monounsaturated fat.

12 (6-inch) corn tortillas, each cut into 6 wedges
   Cooking spray
¼ teaspoon kosher salt, divided
1¼ cups chopped peeled avocado
1 cup chopped peeled mango
1 tablespoon finely chopped fresh cilantro
4 teaspoons fresh lime juice
   Fresh cilantro sprigs (optional)

1. Preheat oven to 425°.
2. Arrange tortilla wedges in a single layer on baking sheets coated with cooking spray. Coat wedges with cooking spray; sprinkle ⅛ teaspoon salt evenly over wedges. Bake at 425° for 8 minutes or until crisp.
3. Combine remaining ⅛ teaspoon salt, avocado, and next 3 ingredients, tossing gently. Let stand 10 minutes. Garnish with cilantro sprigs, if desired. Serve with chips. **Yield:** 9 servings (serving size: about ¼ cup salsa and 8 chips).

CALORIES 123; FAT 4.1g (sat 0.7g, mono 2.3g, poly 0.8g); PROTEIN 2.5g; CARB 21.1g; FIBER 3.2g; CHOL 0mg; IRON 0.8mg; SODIUM 111mg; CALC 65mg

Potato Chips with Blue Cheese Dip

117 calories

This recipe received our Test Kitchens' highest rating. Use a mandoline to cut the potato for the best results; hand-cutting is less likely to produce sufficiently thin and uniform slices. If you have any leftover chips, store them in an airtight container for up to a week. You'll need to bake them for 2 minutes at 450° to recrisp before eating.

⅓ cup (1½ ounces) finely crumbled blue cheese
⅓ cup fat-free sour cream
2 tablespoons light mayonnaise
2 tablespoons fat-free milk
¼ teaspoon Worcestershire sauce
1 pound russet potato, thinly sliced (about 1 large), divided
Cooking spray
½ teaspoon salt, divided

1. Preheat oven to 400°. Place baking sheet in oven.
2. Combine first 5 ingredients in a small bowl, stirring well. Cover and chill.

3. Place potato slices on paper towels; pat dry. Arrange half of potato slices in a single layer on preheated baking sheet coated with cooking spray. Sprinkle with ¼ teaspoon salt. Bake at 400° for 10 minutes. Turn potato slices over; bake an additional 5 minutes or until golden. Repeat procedure with remaining potatoes and remaining ¼ teaspoon salt. Serve immediately with blue cheese mixture. **Yield:** 6 servings (serving size: about ½ cup chips and about 2 tablespoons dip).

CALORIES 117; FAT 3.7g (sat 1.6g, mono 0.6g, poly 0.1g); PROTEIN 4.2g; CARB 16.8g; FIBER 1g; CHOL 9mg; IRON 0.7mg; SODIUM 352mg; CALC 80mg

nutrition note

Baked vs. Fried Potato Chips

Opting to bake potato chips instead of deep-frying them is a healthy switch. You still get the crunch that makes chips so delicious but you save on calories and also particularly on saturated fat. Baked chips contain 74 percent less saturated fat than their fried counterparts.

Indian-Spiced Roasted Nuts

This simple recipe makes a tasty snack. Use your favorite nuts, and add a bit of heat with a dash of ground red pepper, if you like.

120 calories

1½ teaspoons brown sugar
1½ teaspoons honey
  1 teaspoon canola oil
  ¾ teaspoon ground cinnamon
  ⅛ teaspoon salt
  ⅛ teaspoon ground cardamom
  ⅛ teaspoon ground cloves
    Dash of freshly ground black pepper
  ¼ cup blanched almonds
  ¼ cup cashews
  ¼ cup hazelnuts

1. Preheat oven to 350°.
2. Combine first 8 ingredients in a microwave-safe bowl. Microwave at HIGH 30 seconds; stir until blended. Add nuts to sugar mixture; toss to coat.
3. Spread nuts evenly on a baking sheet lined with parchment paper. Bake at 350° for 15 minutes or until golden brown. Cool. **Yield:** 6 servings (serving size: 2 tablespoons).

CALORIES 120; FAT 10g (sat 1g, mono 6.6g, poly 1.8g); PROTEIN 3g; CARB 6.8g; FIBER 1.6g; CHOL 0mg; IRON 1mg; SODIUM 88mg; CALC 28mg

nutrition note

Honey

This wonderfully rich golden liquid is a natural sweetener that can enhance a variety of dishes. The color and flavor of the honey depend on the type of flowers the bees collect the nectar from, but in general, lighter-colored honeys have a milder flavor than darker ones. Research has found that honey contains phytonutrients that have cancer-preventing and anti-tumor qualities. However, a majority of these beneficial compounds can be removed if the honey is heavily processed.

Roasted Chile-Spiced Edamame

113 calories

Frozen edamame that's already been shelled is the key to this recipe's fast prep.

1 **(14-ounce) package frozen shelled edamame (green soybeans), thawed**
Cooking spray
1 **tablespoon New Mexico red chile powder or chili powder**
1 **teaspoon onion powder**
¾ **teaspoon sea salt**
½ **teaspoon ground ginger**
½ **teaspoon ground red pepper**

1. Preheat oven to 350°.
2. Arrange edamame in a single layer on a baking sheet, and coat with cooking spray. Combine chile powder and next 4 ingredients. Sprinkle over edamame; toss to coat.
3. Bake edamame at 350° for 1½ hours, stirring beans every 30 minutes. **Yield:** 5 servings (serving size: about ¼ cup).

CALORIES 113; FAT 3.5g (sat 0.4g, mono 0.7g, poly 1.7g); PROTEIN 8.7g; CARB 10.9g; FIBER 4.8g; CHOL 0mg; IRON 2mg; SODIUM 393mg; CALC 59mg

nutrition note

Edamame

Pronounced eh-dah-MAH-meh, edamame are soybeans that are not fully mature. The bean pod looks like a large, fuzzy sugar snap pea. Whether fresh or frozen, this healthful legume adds fiber, vitamin K, and protein to your diet.

Apricot-Almond Granola

123 calories

Granola makes a great portable snack with lots of fiber and is also good served on yogurt or light ice cream.

2¾ cups old-fashioned rolled oats
½ cup slivered almonds
½ cup dried cherries
½ cup coarsely chopped dried apricots
⅓ cup coarsely chopped walnuts
⅓ cup golden raisins
½ cup honey
⅓ cup butter, melted

1. Preheat oven to 350°.
2. Combine first 6 ingredients in a medium bowl. Combine honey and butter.

Drizzle honey mixture over oat mixture; toss to coat. Spread mixture in a single layer on a jelly-roll pan. Bake at 350° for 15 minutes; stir. Bake an additional 10 minutes or until lightly browned. Cool completely on pan. Break into pieces.
Yield: 6 cups (serving size: ¼ cup).

CALORIES 123; FAT 4.5g (sat 1.5g, mono 1.5g, poly 1.2g); PROTEIN 2.5g; CARB 19.1g; FIBER 2g; CHOL 5mg; IRON 0.8mg; SODIUM 15mg; CALC 19mg

nutrition note

Dried Fruit

Dried fruits (like cranberries, raisins, or apricots) are a sweet way to help you get the two to four servings of fruit you're supposed to have each day. A ¼-cup serving—a small handful—counts as one serving. You'll be getting a dose of vitamins and antioxidants, too.

Maple Kettle Corn

Intensely sweet maple sugar flavors this version of the classic sweet-salty snack. To prevent the sugar from burning, shake the pan as the popcorn cooks.

2 tablespoons canola oil
½ cup unpopped popcorn kernels
¼ cup maple sugar
½ teaspoon kosher salt

1. Heat oil in a 3-quart saucepan over medium-high heat. Add popcorn, sugar, and salt to pan; cover and cook 3 minutes or until kernels begin to pop, shaking pan frequently. Continue cooking 2 minutes, shaking pan constantly to prevent burning. When popping slows down, remove pan from heat. Let stand, covered, until all popping stops. **Yield:** 6 servings (serving size: 2 cups).

CALORIES 119; FAT 5.3g (sat 0.4g, mono 2.8g, poly 1.3g); PROTEIN 1.7g; CARB 16.4g; FIBER 2.4g; CHOL 0mg; IRON 0.4mg; SODIUM 157mg; CALC 5mg

nutrition note

Popcorn

Popcorn has a lot of bulk for its calories, so it helps fill you up. Plus, 3½ cups contains one of your three recommended daily servings of whole grains.

Crisp and Spicy Snack Mix

Make this to snack on before dinner. And if there's any left, toss it on a salad to add crunch.

117 calories

- **2** cups criss-cross of corn and rice cereal (such as Crispix)
- **1** cup tiny pretzel twists
- **½** cup reduced-fat wheat crackers (such as Wheat Thins)
- **½** cup reduced-fat cheddar crackers (such as Cheez-It)
- **1½** tablespoons butter, melted
- **1** tablespoon ginger stir-fry sauce (such as Lawry's)
- **1** teaspoon chili powder
- **1** teaspoon ground cumin
- **¼** teaspoon salt
- Cooking spray

1. Preheat oven to 250°.

2. Combine first 4 ingredients in a bowl. Combine butter and next 4 ingredients; drizzle over cereal mixture, tossing to coat. Spread mixture into a jelly-roll pan coated with cooking spray. Bake at 250° for 30 minutes or until crisp, stirring twice. **Yield:** 4 cups (serving size: ½ cup).

CALORIES 117; FAT 3.9g (sat 1.7g, mono 0.7g, poly 0.5g); PROTEIN 2.2g; CARB 18.5g; FIBER 0.8g; CHOL 6mg; IRON 2.6mg; SODIUM 368mg; CALC 17mg

nutrition note

False Sense of Security

If a snack or dessert is marked as "low-fat," "reduced-fat," or "light," it doesn't necessarily mean it's low in calories. The low-fat claim on the package can sometimes give a false sense of security that these foods are somehow safer to eat, which can lead to overeating. Regardless of fat content, these foods still contain calories, so it's important to treat low-fat foods like any others, and enjoy them in moderation.

Curried Sunflower Brittle

111 calories

If you use color changes as cooking cues for the sunflower seed kernels, curry powder, or sugar mixture, they might become overcooked and bitter. Sugar has no scent until it begins to caramelize; the key to this recipe is adding sunflower seeds right at that point. Store in an airtight container for up to a week.

Cooking spray
1 cup unsalted, untoasted sunflower seed kernels
½ teaspoon curry powder
⅛ teaspoon salt
1¼ cups sugar
¼ cup water
2 tablespoons light-colored corn syrup

1. Line a baking sheet with foil; coat foil with cooking spray. Coat flat surface of a metal spatula with cooking spray; set aside.
2. Heat a large nonstick skillet over medium-high heat. Add kernels; cook until they release a toasted aroma (about 3 minutes), stirring frequently. Place in a bowl; wipe pan with a paper towel.

3. Heat pan over medium-high heat. Add curry powder; cook until fragrant (about 30 seconds), stirring constantly. Add curry to kernels. Sprinkle with salt; stir to combine.
4. Combine sugar, ¼ cup water, and corn syrup in a saucepan. Bring mixture to a boil over medium-high heat, stirring occasionally until sugar dissolves. Continue to cook, without stirring, until first sign of caramel fragrance (about 3 minutes).
5. Remove from heat; stir in kernel mixture. Rapidly spread mixture to about ⅛-inch thickness onto prepared baking sheet using prepared spatula. Cool completely; break into small pieces. **Yield:** 16 servings (serving size: 1 ounce).

CALORIES 111; FAT 3.8g (sat 0.4g, mono 0.7g, poly 2.5g); PROTEIN 1.8g; CARB 19.2g; FIBER 0.8g; CHOL 0mg; IRON 0.5mg; SODIUM 24mg; CALC 11mg

nutrition note

Sunflower Seeds

Like other nuts, sunflower seeds have staying power. Packed with filling protein and healthy fats, these small seeds are also an excellent source of vitamin E, which has antioxidant properties, and contain folate, a vitamin that is necessary for pregnant women to help prevent birth defects.

257

Chocolate Hazelnut Bark

You can substitute any dried fruit in place of the dried cherries in this crunchy, sweet snack.

139 calories

¾ cup hazelnuts (about 4 ounces)
⅓ cup dried cherries, coarsely chopped
2 tablespoons finely chopped crystallized ginger
6 ounces bittersweet chocolate, chopped

1. Preheat oven to 350°.
2. Place hazelnuts on a baking sheet. Bake at 350° for 20 minutes, stirring once halfway through cooking. Turn nuts out onto a towel. Roll up towel; rub off skins. Coarsely chop nuts. Combine chopped nuts, cherries, and ginger in a medium bowl.
3. Place chocolate in a microwave-safe measuring cup. Microwave at HIGH 1 minute or until chocolate melts, stirring every 15 seconds. Add to nut mixture, stirring just until combined. Spread mixture evenly on a jelly-roll pan lined with foil; freeze 1 hour. Break into pieces. **Yield:** About 12 ounces (serving size: 1 ounce).

CALORIES 139; FAT 8.8g (sat 2.5g, mono 3.9g, poly 0.7g); PROTEIN 2.1g; CARB 15.4g; FIBER 1.4g; CHOL 0mg; IRON 0.8mg; SODIUM 5mg; CALC 19mg

nutrition note

Bittersweet Chocolate

This chocolate is a sweetened form of dark chocolate. This type of chocolate contains polyphenols and flavonoids, two types of antioxidants that help prevent damage caused by cholesterol in arteries and may help reduce high blood pressure, reduce LDL cholesterol (the bad kind), or even provide potential cancer-fighting benefits.

Toasted Coconut Marshmallows

107 calories

These are good as a snack or dropped into a mug of hot chocolate. The mixture for the marshmallows becomes quite thick and requires substantial beating time, so you'll want to use a heavy-duty stand mixer instead of a handheld mixer. Using a stand mixer also makes it safer (and easier) to gradually add the hot gelatin mixture to the beaten egg whites. Use a dough scraper to cut the marshmallows into squares with a quick vertical motion (avoid dragging it as you cut the marshmallows). If the dough scraper sticks to the marshmallows, dust it with powdered sugar.

Cooking spray
2 cups flaked sweetened coconut, toasted
2½ envelopes unflavored gelatin (2 tablespoons plus 1¼ teaspoons)
¾ cup cold water, divided
2 cups granulated sugar, divided
⅔ cup light-colored corn syrup
1 tablespoon vanilla extract
¼ teaspoon salt
2 large egg whites
⅔ cup powdered sugar
3 tablespoons cornstarch

1. Line a 13 x 9–inch baking pan with heavy-duty plastic wrap, allowing plastic wrap to extend 1 inch over sides of pan. Lightly coat plastic wrap with cooking spray. Spread coconut in an even layer in bottom of pan; set aside.
2. Sprinkle gelatin over ½ cup cold water in a small bowl; set aside.
3. Combine remaining ¼ cup water, 1¾ cups granulated sugar, and corn syrup in a large saucepan. Cook, without stirring, over medium-high heat until a candy thermometer registers 260° (about 15 minutes). Remove from heat; gradually stir in softened gelatin (mixture will appear foamy).
4. While sugar mixture cooks, beat vanilla, salt, and egg whites using a heavy-duty stand mixer with whisk attachment at high speed until foamy. Gradually add remaining ¼ cup granulated sugar, 1 tablespoon at a time, until stiff peaks form. Gradually pour in gelatin mixture, beating until very thick (about 5 minutes). Gently spread marshmallow mixture over coconut in prepared pan. Coat 1 side of another sheet of plastic wrap with cooking spray. Place plastic wrap, coated side down, over marshmallow mixture. Chill 8 hours or until firm.
5. Sprinkle powdered sugar and cornstarch over a cutting board. Remove top sheet of plastic wrap. Invert marshmallow mixture over powdered sugar mixture. Using a dough scraper, cut mixture into about 1-inch squares. Store between sheets of wax or parchment paper in an airtight container. **Yield:** 8 dozen (serving size: 3 marshmallows).

CALORIES 107; FAT 1.5g (sat 1.3g, mono 0.1g, poly 0g); PROTEIN 0.9g; CARB 23.4g; FIBER 0.2g; CHOL 0mg; IRON 0.1mg; SODIUM 43mg; CALC 2mg

back on track

Don't Deny Yourself

Often weight loss is associated with deprivation, but that method of losing extra pounds may not be the best bet for long-term weight loss and maintenance. When Belgian researchers told 68 women to either enjoy or refuse their favorite snack, the refusers ate more of the forbidden snack once they were given the green light a day later. Sensible snacking helps you avoid overeating.

Deep Dark Chocolate Biscotti

Serve with a cup of coffee for an afternoon pick-me-up. Black coffee doesn't contain many calories—2 calories in an 8-ounce cup—but adding 1 tablespoon of half-and-half (20 calories) and 1 teaspoon of granulated sugar (16 calories) or a sugar substitute will fill out this snack.

9.5	ounces whole-wheat flour (about 2 cups)
2	tablespoons flaxseed
½	teaspoon baking soda
¼	teaspoon salt
⅓	cup granulated sugar
⅓	cup packed dark brown sugar
2	large egg whites
1	large egg
1½	teaspoons vanilla extract
¾	cup unsalted almonds
⅔	cup dark chocolate chips (such as Hershey's)

1. Preheat oven to 350°.
2. Weigh or lightly spoon flour into dry measuring cups; level with a knife. Combine flour and next 3 ingredients in a bowl, stirring with a whisk. Combine granulated sugar and next 3 ingredients in a bowl; beat with a mixer at high speed for 2 minutes. Add vanilla; mix well. Add flour mixture to egg mixture; stir until combined. Fold in almonds and chocolate. Divide dough into 3 equal portions. Roll each portion into a 6-inch-long roll. Arrange rolls 3 inches apart on a baking sheet lined with parchment paper. Pat to 1-inch thickness. Bake at 350° for 28 minutes or until firm.
3. Remove rolls from baking sheet; cool 10 minutes on a wire rack. Cut rolls diagonally into 30 (½-inch) slices. Place, cut sides down, on baking sheet. Reduce oven temperature to 325°; bake 7 minutes. Turn cookies over; bake 7 minutes (cookies will be slightly soft in center but will harden as they cool). Remove from baking sheet; cool on wire rack. **Yield:** 30 servings (serving size: 1 biscotto).

CALORIES 94; FAT 3.5g (sat 0.9g, mono 1.7g, poly 0.7g); PROTEIN 2.7g; CARB 14.4g; FIBER 1.9g; CHOL 7mg; IRON 0.7mg; SODIUM 49mg; CALC 18mg

nutrition note

Whole-Wheat Flour

Whole-wheat flour is more nutritious than refined white flour and using it in baking is one way to incorporate more whole grains into your diet. Processing strips white flour of many of its nutrients, including the fiber, essential fatty acids, and most of the vitamins and minerals, and while some are added back through fortification, it's impossible to replace them all.

Caramel Apple Oatmeal Cookies

83 calories

Dried apples and caramel bits are good replacements for raisins in this version of oatmeal cookies.

6.75 ounces all-purpose flour (about 1½ cups)
1½ cups old-fashioned rolled oats
1 teaspoon baking powder
½ teaspoon baking soda
½ teaspoon salt
¾ cup granulated sugar
¾ cup packed brown sugar
6 tablespoons unsalted butter, softened
2 teaspoons vanilla extract
1 large egg
¾ cup finely chopped dried apple slices
¾ cup caramel bits or 16 small soft caramel candies, chopped

1. Preheat oven to 350°.
2. Weigh or lightly spoon flour into dry measuring cups; level with a knife.

Combine flour and next 4 ingredients in a bowl; stir well.
3. Place sugars and butter in a large bowl; beat with a mixer at medium speed until light and fluffy. Add vanilla and egg; beat well. Gradually add flour mixture; beat at low speed just until combined. Fold in apple and caramel bits.
4. Drop dough by 2 teaspoonfuls 2 inches apart onto baking sheets lined with parchment paper. Flatten balls slightly with hand. Bake at 350° for 9 minutes. Cool on pans 3 minutes. Remove cookies from pans; cool completely on wire racks.
Yield: 4 dozen (serving size: 1 cookie).

CALORIES 83; FAT 2g (sat 1.1g, mono 0.5g, poly 0.3g); PROTEIN 1.1g; CARB 15.5g; FIBER 0.5g; CHOL 8mg; IRON 0.4mg; SODIUM 74mg; CALC 17mg

back on track

Pack a Snack

If you're not snacking, you may want to consider adding one to your day. Eating a snack between meals helps satisfy cravings, keeps your energy and mood high, and provides extra vitamins and minerals that may not be met during meals. Plus, science has found that snacking is good for you. The 5,000-subject-strong National Health and Nutrition Examination Survey found that people who ate snacks in addition to three meals a day had higher levels of nutrients in their diets.

Almond Butter Snickerdoodles

Almond butter puts a modern twist on these classic cookies.

1 cup packed brown sugar
⅓ cup (about 3 ounces) ⅓-less-fat cream cheese, softened
¼ cup unsalted butter, softened
2 tablespoons smooth almond butter
1 teaspoon grated lemon rind
1 teaspoon vanilla extract
2 large egg yolks, lightly beaten
4.75 ounces white whole-wheat flour (about 1 cup)
1.5 ounces whole-wheat flour (about ⅓ cup)
1 teaspoon baking soda
1½ teaspoons ground cinnamon, divided
½ teaspoon salt
2 tablespoons granulated sugar

1. Preheat oven to 350°.

2. Line a large baking sheet with parchment paper.

3. Place first 4 ingredients in a medium bowl, and beat with a mixer at high speed until well combined (about 2 minutes).

Add lemon rind, vanilla, and egg yolks; beat until well blended.

4. Weigh or lightly spoon flours into dry measuring cups; level with a knife. Combine flours, baking soda, ½ teaspoon cinnamon, and salt; stir with a whisk. Add flour mixture to butter mixture; beat at low speed until well combined. Drop half of dough by rounded tablespoonfuls onto prepared baking sheet. Combine remaining 1 teaspoon cinnamon and granulated sugar in a small bowl; sprinkle half of cinnamon-sugar mixture evenly over cookies. Bake at 350° for 6 minutes; flatten cookies with back of a spatula. Bake an additional 6 minutes. Cool on pans 1 minute. Remove from pans, and cool on wire racks. Repeat procedure with remaining dough and sugar mixture. **Yield:** 2 dozen (serving size: 1 cookie).

CALORIES 104; FAT 3.8g (sat 1.9g, mono 1.2g, poly 0.3g); PROTEIN 1.6g; CARB 16.2g; FIBER 0.5g; CHOL 25mg; IRON 0.7mg; SODIUM 127mg; CALC 19mg

nutrition note

Almond Butter

Like other nut butters, almonds butter retains the nutrients of almonds, which means it's rich in protein, fiber, and healthy fats. Two tablespoons of almond butter also provides 30 percent of daily magnesium needs and is a rich source of vitamin E. This satisfying spread comes in two varieties, raw and roasted. Use raw for a subtle, sweet taste and roasted for more intense flavor.

Chocolate Chip Cookies

Store up to one week in an airtight container—if they last that long. We suggest keeping a dozen in the freezer for emergencies.

88 calories

10 ounces all-purpose flour (about 2¼ cups)
 1 teaspoon baking soda
 ¼ teaspoon salt
 1 cup packed brown sugar
 ¾ cup granulated sugar
 ½ cup butter, softened
 1 teaspoon vanilla extract
 2 large egg whites
 ¾ cup semisweet chocolate chips
   Cooking spray

1. Preheat oven to 350°.
2. Weigh or lightly spoon flour into dry measuring cups; level with a knife. Combine flour, baking soda, and salt, stirring with a whisk.

3. Combine sugars and butter in a large bowl; beat with a mixer at medium speed until well blended. Add vanilla and egg whites; beat 1 minute. Add flour mixture and chips; beat until blended.
4. Drop dough by level tablespoons 2 inches apart onto baking sheets coated with cooking spray. Bake at 350° for 10 minutes or until lightly browned. Cool on pans 2 minutes. Remove from pans; cool completely on wire racks. **Yield:** 4 dozen (serving size: 1 cookie).

CALORIES 88; FAT 3g (sat 1.8g, mono 0.5g, poly 0.1g); PROTEIN 1g; CARB 14.6g; FIBER 0.2g; CHOL 5mg; IRON 0.4mg; SODIUM 56mg; CALC 5mg

back on track

Pre-Portion Tempting Treats

The bigger the package, the more food you'll pour out of it. When two groups were given half- or 1-pound bags of M&Ms to eat while watching TV, those given the 1-pound bag ate nearly twice as much. When you make a batch of snacks or treats, divide it into servings and place each in its own zip-top plastic bag or wrap it individually in plastic wrap.

Mudslide Cookies

When the cookies are done, they'll be cracked on top and still moist in the center.

2 ounces bittersweet chocolate, coarsely chopped
2 ounces unsweetened chocolate, coarsely chopped
1½ tablespoons butter
1 tablespoon instant coffee granules
1 tablespoon hot water
1 teaspoon vanilla extract
6.75 ounces all-purpose flour (about 1½ cups)
½ cup unsweetened cocoa
2 teaspoons baking powder
⅛ teaspoon salt
2½ cups sugar
½ cup egg substitute
2 large eggs
½ cup chopped walnuts
¼ cup semisweet chocolate minichips

1. Preheat oven to 350°.
2. Place first 3 ingredients in a microwave-safe bowl; microwave at HIGH 1 minute or until chocolate is almost melted. Stir until smooth.
3. Combine coffee granules and 1 tablespoon hot water, stirring until granules dissolve. Stir coffee and vanilla into chocolate mixture.
4. Weigh or lightly spoon flour into dry measuring cups; level with a knife. Combine flour and next 3 ingredients, stirring well with a whisk. Combine sugar, egg substitute, and eggs in a large bowl; beat with a mixer at high speed 6 minutes or until thick and pale. Gently stir one-fourth of egg mixture into chocolate mixture; stir chocolate mixture into remaining egg mixture. Stir in flour mixture, nuts, and chocolate chips.
5. Cover baking sheets with parchment paper. Drop dough by rounded tablespoonfuls 2 inches apart on prepared baking sheets; with moist hands, gently press dough into ¼-inch-thick rounds. Bake at 350° for 15 minutes or until set. Cool 1 minute. Remove from pans; cool completely on wire racks. **Yield:** 30 servings (serving size: 1 cookie).

CALORIES 142; FAT 4.7g (sat 2g, mono 1g, poly 1.1g); PROTEIN 2.5g; CARB 25.2g; FIBER 1.3g; CHOL 16mg; IRON 1.1mg; SODIUM 59mg; CALC 29mg

quick fix

Soccer

A casual game of soccer with friends can be a fun way to exercise. Thirty minutes on the field can burn 250 calories. If it's a competitive game with lots of running, that number can increase to 350 calories in 30 minutes.

Espresso Crinkles

Lightly coat your hands with flour to make rolling the dough into balls easier. The dough freezes well. Freeze the dough after step 1, thaw in the refrigerator, then proceed with step 2. The powdered sugar coating gives these cookies an appealing cracked finish. Serve with coffee to echo the espresso flavor.

4.5   **ounces all-purpose flour (about 1 cup)**

1¼   **cups powdered sugar, divided**

¼   **cup unsweetened cocoa**

1¼   **teaspoons baking powder**

⅛   **teaspoon salt**

5¼   **teaspoons canola oil**

1½   **ounces unsweetened chocolate, chopped**

1   **teaspoon instant espresso granules**

¾   **cup packed brown sugar**

3   **tablespoons light-colored corn syrup**

1½   **teaspoons vanilla extract**

2   **large egg whites**

1. Weigh or lightly spoon flour into a dry measuring cup; level with a knife. Combine flour, ¾ cup powdered sugar, and next 3 ingredients in a medium bowl; stir with a whisk. Combine oil and chocolate in a small saucepan over low heat; cook until chocolate melts, stirring constantly. Add espresso granules to pan; stir until blended. Remove from heat. Pour chocolate mixture into a large bowl; cool 5 minutes. Stir in brown sugar, syrup, and vanilla. Add egg whites, stirring with a whisk. Add flour mixture to egg mixture, stirring gently just until combined. Cover; chill at least 2 hours or overnight.

2. Preheat oven to 350°.

3. Roll dough into 1-inch balls. Dredge balls in remaining ½ cup powdered sugar; place balls 2 inches apart on 2 baking sheets lined with parchment paper. Bake at 350° for 10 minutes or until tops are cracked and almost set. Cool cookies on pan 2 minutes or until set; remove from pan. Cool cookies on a wire rack. **Yield:** 24 servings (serving size: 1 cookie).

CALORIES 98; FAT 2g (sat 0.6g, mono 0.6g, poly 0.3g); PROTEIN 1.2g; CARB 19.5g; FIBER 0.6g; CHOL 0mg; IRON 0.7mg; SODIUM 47mg; CALC 21mg

quick fix

Golf

A game of golf with friends can be a social and enjoyable way to exercise. You can burn more than 250 calories in an hour—even more if you walk more than you ride in the golf cart.

Cranberry-Oatmeal Bars

These cranberry-oatmeal bar cookies strike a nice flavor balance: not too sweet and not too tart. Be sure to zest the orange before you squeeze the juice.

CRUST

- 4.5 ounces all-purpose flour (about 1 cup)
- 1 cup quick-cooking oats
- ½ cup packed brown sugar
- ¼ teaspoon salt
- ¼ teaspoon baking soda
- ¼ teaspoon ground cinnamon
- 6 tablespoons butter, melted
- 3 tablespoons orange juice
- Cooking spray

FILLING

- 1⅓ cups dried cranberries (about 6 ounces)
- ¾ cup sour cream
- ½ cup granulated sugar
- 2 tablespoons all-purpose flour
- 1 teaspoon vanilla extract
- ½ teaspoon grated orange rind
- 1 large egg white, lightly beaten

1. Preheat oven to 325°.

2. To prepare crust, weigh or lightly spoon flour into a dry measuring cup; level with a knife. Combine flour and next 5 ingredients in a medium bowl, stirring well with a whisk. Drizzle butter and juice over flour mixture, stirring until moistened (mixture will be crumbly). Reserve ½ cup oat mixture. Press remaining oat mixture into bottom of an 11 x 7–inch baking dish coated with cooking spray.

3. To prepare filling, combine cranberries and next 6 ingredients in a medium bowl, stirring well. Spread cranberry mixture over prepared crust; sprinkle reserved oat mixture evenly over filling. Bake at 325° for 40 minutes or until edges are golden. Cool completely in pan on a wire rack. **Yield:** 24 servings (serving size: 1 square).

CALORIES 133; FAT 4.6g (sat 2.6g, mono 0.8g, poly 0.2g); PROTEIN 1.5g; CARB 21.9g; FIBER 0.9g; CHOL 13mg; IRON 0.6mg; SODIUM 67mg; CALC 20mg

Cherry-Oatmeal Bars: Substitute dried cherries for the dried cranberries and lemon rind for the orange rind in the filling.

CALORIES 135; FAT 4.6g (sat 2.6g, mono 0.8g, poly 0.2g); PROTEIN 1.7g; CARB 21.5g; FIBER 1.3g; CHOL 13mg; IRON 0.7mg; SODIUM 68mg; CALC 27mg

Maple-Date-Oatmeal Bars: Substitute chopped pitted dates for the dried cranberries. Omit granulated sugar from filling, and add 2 tablespoons maple syrup and 2 tablespoons brown sugar.

CALORIES 124; FAT 4.6g (sat 2.6g, mono 0.8g, poly 0.2g); PROTEIN 1.7g; CARB 19.8g; FIBER 1.1g; CHOL 13mg; IRON 0.7mg; SODIUM 68mg; CALC 26mg

quick fix

Fall Leaves

When your lawn is littered with leaves in the fall, grab a rake and go to it. You'll get the benefit of exercise—you can burn 280 calories in 30 minutes—and a beautiful lawn.

Butterscotch Bars

A small square of these rich bars is enough to satisfy a dessert craving. The flour and oats mixture is somewhat dry after combining, but it serves as both a solid base for the soft butterscotch chip layer and a crumbly, streusel-like topping.

148 calories

  1 **cup packed brown sugar**
  5 **tablespoons butter, melted**
  1 **teaspoon vanilla extract**
  1 **large egg, lightly beaten**
  9 **ounces all-purpose flour (about 2 cups)**
2½ **cups quick-cooking oats**
  ½ **teaspoon salt**
  ½ **teaspoon baking soda**
    Cooking spray
  ¾ **cup fat-free sweetened condensed milk**
1¼ **cups butterscotch morsels (about 8 ounces)**
  ⅛ **teaspoon salt**
  ½ **cup finely chopped walnuts, toasted**

1. Preheat oven to 350°.
2. Combine sugar and butter in a large bowl. Stir in vanilla and egg. Weigh or lightly spoon flour into dry measuring cups; level with a knife. Combine flour and next 3 ingredients in a bowl. Add oat mixture to sugar mixture; stir with a fork until combined (mixture will be crumbly). Place 3 cups oat mixture in bottom of a 13 x 9–inch baking pan coated with cooking spray; press into bottom of pan. Set aside.
3. Place condensed milk, butterscotch morsels, and ⅛ teaspoon salt in a microwave-safe bowl; microwave at HIGH 1 minute or until butterscotch morsels melt, stirring every 20 seconds. Stir in walnuts. Scrape mixture into pan, spreading evenly over crust. Sprinkle evenly with remaining oat mixture, gently pressing into butterscotch mixture. Bake at 350° for 30 minutes or until topping is golden brown. Place pan on a wire rack; run a knife around outside edge. Cool completely. Cut into 36 bars. **Yield:** 36 servings (serving size: 1 bar).

CALORIES 148; FAT 5.1g (sat 2.7g, mono 0.9g, poly 1.1g); PROTEIN 2.6g; CARB 23.4g; FIBER 0.8g; CHOL 11mg; IRON 0.8mg; SODIUM 87mg; CALC 31mg

nutrition note

Sweetened Condensed Milk

Sweetened condensed milk is cow's milk from which water has been removed and sugar has been added. The result is a thick, sweet milk that adds richness to a variety of dishes, particularly desserts. For a healthier alternative to the whole-milk version, there are low-fat and fat-free varieties that provide significant saturated-fat savings—regular sweetened condensed milk has 16 grams per cup, while the low-fat variety contains 8 grams and the fat-free version has 0 grams.

Vanilla Bean Shortbread

You can make these cookies up to five days ahead, and store them in an airtight container.

Cooking spray
9   ounces all-purpose flour (about
    2 cups)
¼   cup cornstarch
¼   teaspoon salt
½   cup butter, softened
½   cup canola oil
½   cup sugar
1   vanilla bean, split lengthwise

1. Preheat oven to 350°.
2. Line bottom and sides of a 13 x 9–inch baking pan with foil; coat foil with cooking spray, and set aside.
3. Weigh or lightly spoon flour into dry measuring cups; level with a knife. Combine flour, cornstarch, and salt in a large bowl; stir with a whisk.
4. Place butter in a medium bowl; beat with a mixer at medium speed 2 minutes or until light and fluffy. Add oil; beat with a mixer at medium speed 3 minutes or until well blended. Gradually add sugar, beating well. Scrape seeds from vanilla bean, and add seeds to butter mixture; discard bean. Add flour mixture, beating at low speed just until blended. Spoon dough into prepared pan. Place a sheet of heavy-duty plastic wrap over dough; press to an even thickness. Discard plastic wrap. Bake at 350° for 30 minutes or until edges are lightly browned. Cool in pan 5 minutes on a wire rack; cut into 32 pieces. Carefully lift foil from pan; cool squares completely on wire rack.
Yield: 32 servings (serving size: 1 piece).

CALORIES 101; FAT 6.4g (sat 2.1g, mono 2.8g, poly 1.2g); PROTEIN 0.9g; CARB 10.1g; FIBER 0.2g; CHOL 8mg; IRON 0.4mg SODIUM 39mg; CALC 2mg

nutrition note

A Lighter Shortbread

Rich, buttery shortbread is traditionally high in saturated fat, but it can be made lighter. In this recipe, we've replaced half of the butter used in traditional recipes with canola oil, which is rich in heart-healthy un-saturated fat. It's a simple change that makes our version a lot better for you and cuts the saturated fat in half.

Fudgy Mocha-Toffee Brownies

These gooey bars are as rich as anything you'll find in a bakery. They are a welcome treat in a lunch box, as a weeknight dessert, or any time you need a sweet treat.

Cooking spray
2 tablespoons instant coffee granules
¼ cup hot water
¼ cup butter
¼ cup semisweet chocolate chips
6.75 ounces all-purpose flour (about 1½ cups)
1⅓ cups sugar
½ cup unsweetened cocoa
1 teaspoon baking powder
½ teaspoon salt
1 teaspoon vanilla extract
2 large eggs
¼ cup toffee chips

1. Preheat oven to 350°.
2. Coat bottom of a 9-inch square baking pan with cooking spray.
3. Combine coffee granules and ¼ cup hot water, stirring until coffee granules dissolve.

4. Combine butter and chocolate chips in a small microwave-safe bowl. Microwave at HIGH 1 minute or until butter melts; stir until chocolate is smooth.
5. Weigh or lightly spoon flour into dry measuring cups; level with a knife. Combine flour and next 4 ingredients in a large bowl, stirring with a whisk. Combine coffee mixture, butter mixture, vanilla, and eggs in a medium bowl, stirring with a whisk. Add coffee mixture to flour mixture; stir just until combined. Spread evenly into prepared pan. Sprinkle evenly with toffee chips. Bake at 350° for 22 minutes. Cool on a wire rack. **Yield:** 20 servings (serving size: 1 brownie).

CALORIES 145; FAT 4.8g (sat 2.4g, mono 1.8g, poly 0.3g); PROTEIN 2.2g; CARB 24.9g; FIBER 1.1g; CHOL 30mg; IRON 0.9mg; SODIUM 121mg; CALC 23mg

back on track

Join a League

Many cities offer adult league team sports where games are played on weeknights or weekends or both depending on the league. From softball and soccer to rugby and lacrosse, you're bound to find something you're interested in, and many also divide teams into brackets based on skill level, so even beginners can join in and compete against other beginners. So, gather your friends and sign up to add some variety to your exercise routine.

Cream Cheese–Swirled Brownies

131 calories

For moist and fudgy results, be careful not to overbake. When the brownies are perfectly done, the edges of the batter will just begin to pull away from the pan.

- **6.75 ounces all-purpose flour (about 1½ cups)**
- **2 cups sugar, divided**
- **½ cup unsweetened cocoa**
- **½ teaspoon baking powder**
- **¼ teaspoon salt**
- **¼ cup butter**
- **2 ounces unsweetened chocolate, chopped**
- **¾ cup 2% reduced-fat milk**
- **¾ teaspoon vanilla extract, divided**
- **2 large eggs**
- **Cooking spray**
- **½ cup (4 ounces) ⅓-less-fat cream cheese, softened**
- **1 large egg white**

1. Preheat oven to 350°.

2. Weigh or lightly spoon flour into dry measuring cups; level with a knife. Combine flour, 1¾ cups sugar, cocoa, baking powder, and salt in a large bowl, stirring well with a whisk. Place butter and chocolate in a microwave-safe bowl; microwave at HIGH 45 seconds or until melted, stirring once. Combine milk, ½ teaspoon vanilla, and eggs, stirring well with a whisk. Add chocolate mixture and milk mixture to flour mixture; beat with a mixer at medium speed until blended. Spoon batter evenly into a 13 x 9–inch baking pan coated with cooking spray.

3. Place remaining ¼ cup sugar, remaining ¼ teaspoon vanilla, cheese, and egg white in a medium bowl; beat at medium speed until well blended using clean, dry beaters. Drizzle cheese mixture evenly over chocolate mixture; swirl batters together using tip of a knife. Bake at 350° for 30 minutes or until batter begins to pull away from sides of pan. Cool completely on a wire rack. **Yield:** 28 servings (serving size: 1 brownie).

CALORIES 131; FAT 4.3g (sat 2.6g, mono 1.3g, poly 0.2g); PROTEIN 2.5g; CARB 21.5g; FIBER 0.8g; CHOL 23mg; IRON 1.3mg; SODIUM 69mg; CALC 23mg

nutrition note

Cream Cheese

Opting to use ⅓-less-fat cream cheese is a good middle-of-the-road option. In addition to being lower in saturated fat, it contains about 30 percent fewer calories than the full-fat variety while still providing a creamy texture and rich mouthfeel.

Zucchini-Pineapple Quick Bread

146 calories

This recipe makes two loaves. Freeze the extra loaf, tightly wrapped in plastic wrap and heavy-duty foil, for up to one month. Thaw at room temperature. Slices are good microwaved at HIGH 10 to 15 seconds.

13.5   ounces sifted all-purpose flour (about 3 cups)
1½   teaspoons ground cinnamon
 1   teaspoon salt
 1   teaspoon baking soda
 ½   teaspoon baking powder
 2   large eggs
 2   cups sugar
 2   cups grated zucchini (about 1½ medium zucchini)
 ⅔   cup canola oil
 ½   cup egg substitute
 2   teaspoons vanilla extract
 2   (8-ounce) cans crushed pineapple in juice, drained
     Baking spray with flour

1. Preheat oven to 325°.
2. Weigh or lightly spoon flour into dry measuring cups; level with a knife.

Combine flour and next 4 ingredients in a large bowl, stirring well with a whisk.
3. Beat eggs with a mixer at medium speed until foamy. Add sugar and next 4 ingredients, beating until well blended. Add zucchini mixture to flour mixture, stirring just until moist. Fold in pineapple. Spoon batter into 2 (9 x 5–inch) loaf pans coated with baking spray. Bake at 325° for 1 hour or until a wooden pick inserted in center comes out clean. Cool 10 minutes in pans on a wire rack; remove from pans. Cool completely on wire rack. **Yield:** 2 loaves, 16 servings per loaf (serving size: 1 slice).

CALORIES 146; FAT 5.2g (sat 0.4g, mono 2.9g, poly 1.5g); PROTEIN 2.1g; CARB 23.2g; FIBER 0.6g; CHOL 13mg; IRON 0.8mg; SODIUM 132mg; CALC 14mg

nutrition note

Zucchini

Although readily available throughout the year, zucchini is at its peak from May through July. This richly colored green vegetable contains vitamins C and A, potassium, folate, and fiber.

Kalamata Olive Bread with Oregano

133 calories

1 tablespoon olive oil
1 cup finely chopped onion
9 ounces all-purpose flour (about 2 cups)
1 teaspoon baking soda
½ teaspoon salt
1 cup low-fat buttermilk
2 tablespoons butter, melted
2 large egg whites
¼ cup pitted kalamata olives, chopped
1 tablespoon chopped fresh oregano
Cooking spray

1. Preheat oven to 350°.
2. Heat oil in a large nonstick skillet over medium-high heat. Add onion to pan; sauté 3 minutes or until onion is tender. Set aside.
3. Weigh or lightly spoon flour into dry measuring cups; level with a knife.

Combine flour, baking soda, and salt in a large bowl; make a well in center of mixture. Combine buttermilk, butter, and egg whites, stirring with a whisk. Add buttermilk mixture to flour mixture, stirring just until moist. Fold in onion, olives, and oregano.
4. Spread batter into an 8 x 4–inch loaf pan coated with cooking spray. Bake at 350° for 45 minutes or until a wooden pick inserted in center comes out clean. Cool 10 minutes in pan on a wire rack; remove from pan. Cool completely on wire rack. **Yield:** 12 servings (serving size: 1 slice).

CALORIES 133; FAT 4.6g (sat 1.8g, mono 2.2g, poly 0.4g); PROTEIN 3.8g; CARB 18.8g; FIBER 0.8g; CHOL 6.7mg; IRON 1mg; SODIUM 302mg; CALC 39mg

nutrition note

Olives

Olives deliver big flavor in a small package. This fruit can help satisfy a salty craving while offering nutritional benefits to boot. The majority of fat—88 percent— found in olives is the healthy unsaturated variety.

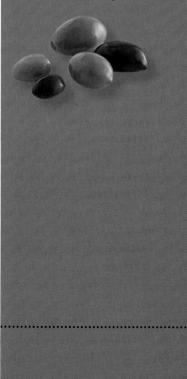

Cucumber, Apple, and Mint Cooler

91 calories

Each serving of this smoothie offers a half-cup of vegetables, plus a little fruit.

1 cup chopped seeded peeled cucumber (about ½ pound)
⅓ cup unsweetened frozen 100% apple juice concentrate, undiluted
¼ cup cold water
¼ cup chopped fresh mint
10 ice cubes (about 4 ounces)
 Cucumber slices (optional)

1. Place first 5 ingredients in a blender; process 2 minutes or until smooth. Garnish with cucumber slices, if desired. Serve immediately. **Yield:** 2 servings (serving size: 1 cup).

CALORIES 91; FAT 0.4g (sat 0.1g, mono 0g, poly 0.1g); PROTEIN 1g; CARB 21.6g; FIBER 1.4g; CHOL 0mg; IRON 2mg; SODIUM 16mg; CALC 41mg

nutrition note

Fruit Juice Concentrate

Juice made from concentrate is the same as the original juice—the only thing that is missing is a majority of the water. Removing the water reduces the volume and weight of the juice, which makes it easier to ship. When water is added back to concentrate, the reconstituted juice generally has the same nutrition profile as the original juice. (The exception is if sugar is added when the juice is reconstituted.) Make sure you buy ones labeled "100 percent juice" to get all the nutritional benefits.

Carrot, Apple, and Ginger Refresher

138 calories

This quick and easy drink is slim on saturated fat.

½ **cup 100% carrot juice, chilled**
½ **cup unsweetened applesauce**
½ **cup organic vanilla fat-free yogurt**
1 **teaspoon fresh lemon juice**
½ **teaspoon grated peeled fresh ginger**
1 **frozen sliced ripe banana**
5 **ice cubes (about 2 ounces)**

1. Place all ingredients in a blender; process 2 minutes or until smooth. Serve immediately. **Yield:** 2 servings (serving size: about 1¼ cups).

CALORIES 138; FAT 0.1g (sat 0g, mono 0g, poly 0.1g); PROTEIN 4.3g; CARB 32.7g; FIBER 2.3g; CHOL 2mg; IRON 0.3mg; SODIUM 79mg; CALC 126mg

nutrition note

Fresh Ginger

Ginger has a warm, slightly woody flavor that adds a subtle sweetness to dishes. Like other spices, it's an ideal way to add loads of flavor without adding many (if any) calories or sodium.

Mango Lassi

This sweet, Indian-style, smoothie-like drink is a blend of fresh mango, tangy plain yogurt, and milk. Choose low-fat or fat-free dairy products to keep saturated fat in check while delivering healthful calcium, potassium, and vitamin D.

137 calories

- 1 **cup chopped fresh mango**
- 1½ **tablespoons sugar**
- 1½ **cups plain fat-free Greek yogurt**
- ½ **cup 1% low-fat milk**
- 2 **teaspoons chopped pistachios**
- **Dash of ground cardamom (optional)**

1. Place mango and sugar in a blender; process until pureed. Add yogurt and milk; process until smooth. Serve with pistachios; sprinkle with cardamom, if desired. **Yield:** 3 servings (serving size: 1 cup lassi and about ½ teaspoon pistachios).

CALORIES 137; FAT 1.4g (sat 0.4g, mono 0.6g, poly 0.3g); PROTEIN 7g; CARB 27.5g; FIBER 1.2g; CHOL 4mg; IRON 0.2mg; SODIUM 89mg; CALC 207mg

nutrition note

Greek Yogurt

Greek yogurt is strained to remove most of the liquid or whey, which results in a deliciously thick yogurt that helps make this Mango Lassi creamy. Greek yogurt contains more protein than regular fat-free yogurt—about 7 more grams per 5.3-ounce carton—and less sodium, but it also contains less calcium. Regular fat-free yogurt has three times more calcium than Greek yogurt.

Lemonade Iced Tea Sorbet

104 calories

Full-flavored English Breakfast tea is usually made from a blend that includes black tea leaves. But consider substituting your favorite tea to make this refreshing sorbet.

2 cups boiling water
4 regular-sized English Breakfast tea bags
¾ cup sugar
¾ cup fresh lemon juice (about 4 lemons)
1 cup ice water
Mint sprigs (optional)
Lemon slices (optional)

1. Combine 2 cups boiling water and tea bags in a large bowl; steep 5 minutes. Discard tea bags. Add sugar to tea mixture, stirring until sugar dissolves. Cool completely. Stir in juice and 1 cup ice water; chill 1 hour.

2. Pour tea mixture into freezer can of an ice-cream freezer; freeze according to manufacturer's instructions. Spoon sorbet into a freezer-safe container. Cover and freeze 1 hour or until firm. Garnish with mint sprigs and lemon slices, if desired.

Yield: 6 servings (serving size: ⅔ cup).

CALORIES 104; FAT 0g (sat 0g, mono 0g, poly 0g); PROTEIN 0.1g; CARB 27.6g; FIBER 0.1g; CHOL 0mg; IRON 0mg; SODIUM 0mg; CALC 2mg

nutrition note

Tea

Normal tea blends as well as green and black teas contain polyphenols and flavonoids—naturally occurring compounds that have antioxidant properties. These compounds may play a role in reducing the risk of heart disease, heart attack, and stroke, and lowering the risk for certain types of cancers.

Cranberry-Jalapeño Granita

Remove the jalapeño seeds if you prefer a milder dessert. You could also use this spicy-sweet ice to top oysters on the half shell.

2 cups cranberry juice cocktail
⅓ cup sugar
4 (5-inch) mint sprigs (about ½ ounce)
1 jalapeño pepper, sliced
2 tablespoons fresh lime juice

1. Combine first 4 ingredients in a small saucepan; bring to a boil. Cover and remove from heat; let stand 15 minutes. Strain cranberry mixture through a fine mesh sieve into an 11 x 7–inch baking dish; discard solids. Cool to room temperature; stir in lime juice. Cover and freeze about 45 minutes. Stir cranberry mixture every 45 minutes until completely frozen (about 3 hours). Remove mixture from freezer; scrape entire mixture with a fork until fluffy. **Yield:** 4 servings (serving size: ½ cup).

CALORIES 135; FAT 0.1g (sat 0g, mono 0g, poly 0.1g); PROTEIN 0.1g; CARB 34.5g; FIBER 0.1g; CHOL 0mg; IRON 0.3mg; SODIUM 3mg; CALC 7mg

nutrition note

Jalapeños

In addition to adding a fiery bite—but relatively few calories—to dishes (1 pepper contains about 4 calories), jalapeños contain vitamin C, vitamin A, and folate.

Nutritional Analysis

How to Use It and Why

Glance at the end of any *Cooking Light* recipe, and you'll see how committed we are to helping you make the best of today's light cooking. With chefs, registered dietitians, home economists, and a computer system that analyzes every ingredient we use, *Cooking Light* gives you authoritative dietary detail like no other magazine. We go to such lengths so you can see how our recipes fit into your healthful eating plan. If you're trying to lose weight, the calorie and fat figures will probably help most. But if you're keeping a close eye on the sodium, cholesterol, and saturated fat in your diet, we provide those numbers, too. And because many women don't get enough iron or calcium, we can help there, as well. Finally, there's a fiber analysis for those of us who don't get enough roughage.

Here's a helpful guide to put our nutritional analysis numbers into perspective. Remember, one size doesn't fit all, so take your lifestyle, age, and circumstances into consideration when determining your nutrition needs. For example, pregnant or breast-feeding women need more protein, calories, and calcium. And women older than 50 need 1,200mg of calcium daily, 200mg more than the amount recommended for younger women.

In Our Nutritional Analysis, We Use These Abbreviations

sat	saturated fat	**CHOL**	cholesterol
mono	monounsaturated fat	**CALC**	calcium
poly	polyunsaturated fat	**g**	gram
CARB	carbohydrates	**mg**	milligram

Daily Nutrition Guide

	Women Ages 25 to 50	Women over 50	Men over 24
Calories	2,000	2,000 or less	2,700
Protein	50g	50g or less	63g
Fat	65g or less	65g or less	88g or less
Saturated Fat	20g or less	20g or less	27g or less
Carbohydrates	304g	304g	410g
Fiber	25g to 35g	25g to 35g	25g to 35g
Cholesterol	300mg or less	300mg or less	300mg or less
Iron	18mg	8mg	8mg
Sodium	2,300mg or less	1,500mg or less	2,300mg or less
Calcium	1,000mg	1,200mg	1,000mg

The nutritional values used in our calculations either come from The Food Processor, Version 8.9 (ESHA Research), or are provided by food manufacturers.

Metric Equivalents

The information in the following charts is provided to help cooks outside the United States successfully use the recipes in this book. All equivalents are approximate.

Cooking/Oven Temperatures

	Fahrenheit	Celsius	Gas Mark
Freeze Water	32° F	0° C	
Room Temp.	68° F	20° C	
Boil Water	212° F	100° C	
Bake	325° F	160° C	3
	350° F	180° C	4
	375° F	190° C	5
	400° F	200° C	6
	425° F	220° C	7
	450° F	230° C	8
Broil			Grill

Liquid Ingredients by Volume

¼ tsp	=					1 ml
½ tsp	=					2 ml
1 tsp	=					5 ml
3 tsp	=	1 tbl	=	½ floz	=	15 ml
2 tbls	=	⅛ cup	=	1 floz	=	30 ml
4 tbls	=	¼ cup	=	2 floz	=	60 ml
5⅓ tbls	=	⅓ cup	=	3 floz	=	80 ml
8 tbls	=	½ cup	=	4 floz	=	120 ml
10⅔ tbls	=	⅔ cup	=	5 floz	=	160 ml
12 tbls	=	¾ cup	=	6 floz	=	180 ml
16 tbls	=	1 cup	=	8 floz	=	240 ml
1 pt	=	2 cups	=	16 floz	=	480 ml
1 qt	=	4 cups	=	32 floz	=	960 ml
				33 floz	=	1000 ml = 1 l

Dry Ingredients by Weight

(To convert ounces to grams, multiply the number of ounces by 30.)

1 oz	=	¹⁄₁₆ lb	=	30 g
4 oz	=	¼ lb	=	120 g
8 oz	=	½ lb	=	240 g
12 oz	=	¾ lb	=	360 g
16 oz	=	1 lb	=	480 g

Length

(To convert inches to centimeters, multiply the number of inches by 2.5.)

1 in	=			2.5 cm	
6 in	=	½ ft	=	15 cm	
12 in	=	1 ft	=	30 cm	
36 in	=	3 ft = 1 yd	=	90 cm	
40 in	=			100 cm	= 1 m

Equivalents for Different Types of Ingredients

Standard Cup	Fine Powder (ex. flour)	Grain (ex. rice)	Granular (ex. sugar)	Liquid Solids (ex. butter)	Liquid (ex. milk)
1	140 g	150 g	190 g	200 g	240 ml
¾	105 g	113 g	143 g	150 g	180 ml
⅔	93 g	100 g	125 g	133 g	160 ml
½	70 g	75 g	95 g	100 g	120 ml
⅓	47 g	50 g	63 g	67 g	80 ml
¼	35 g	38 g	48 g	50 g	60 ml
⅛	18 g	19 g	24 g	25 g	30 ml

index